JOHN SMITH? –
NO PROBLEM!!!!!

My Grandfather, Ernest William Smith, Sergeant, Royal Field Artillery, was said to have come from Croydon, married my Grandmother in Tiverton, Devon, was gassed during the 1914–18 War and died when my Father was aged seven. That was all that was known of him. Just that – no dates, no service number, nothing more. Yet we managed to find out who he was and to trace his family from county to county, back through the centuries to 1497. This is the story of that search, a search made possible by a wide range of sources and accomplished with the help of several different methods, which were, as far as we know, of our own devising and are described herein, that others may make use of them. Chapter by chapter, we reach back through the years, from the 1914–18 War to the reign of King Henry VIII and edge just that little bit further, into the remoter past, introducing you to a miscellany of facts, such as terms once used and practices commonplace in earlier centuries, as we retrace the steps which led us to our many Smith forefathers, who have come to mean so much more to us than just a name on paper. That that name turned out to be John Smith, on not just the one occasion, but five, meant that we had to try to do the impossible. This is how we did it!

L. Welsford

GU00778413

JOHN SMITH? – NO PROBLEM!!!!!

L. & A. Welsford

ARTHUR H. STOCKWELL LTD
Torrs Park, Ilfracombe, Devon, EX34 8BA
Established 1898
www.ahstockwell.co.uk

British Library Cataloguing-in-Publication Data.
A catalogue record for this book is available
from the British Library.

FRONT COVER – Document reproduced by
kind permission of the President and Fellows of
Magdalen College, Oxford.

ISBN 978-0-7223-4510-8
Printed in Great Britain by
Arthur H. Stockwell Ltd
Torrs Park   Ilfracombe
Devon EX34 8BA

Dedicated to Jack Ernest Smith

With special thanks to –

Paul Evans, librarian, Firepower, The Royal Artillery Museum, Woolwich, without whom this could never have been written.

Chris Bennett, Archivist, Croydon Local Studies Library (now Museum of Croydon), whose help in caring for and providing the schools records was invaluable to us.

Dr Robin Darwall-Smith, Archivist, Magdalen College, Oxford, for opening such a warm and welcoming door to the more distant past and for his kind help in providing a wealth of documents, some at his own suggestion, and in reading almost indecipherable entries.

Andrew Mussell, Archivist, Lincoln College, Oxford, for his immeasurable help.

And the staff of the Surrey History Centre, the Centre for Buckinghamshire Studies and the Oxfordshire History Centre.

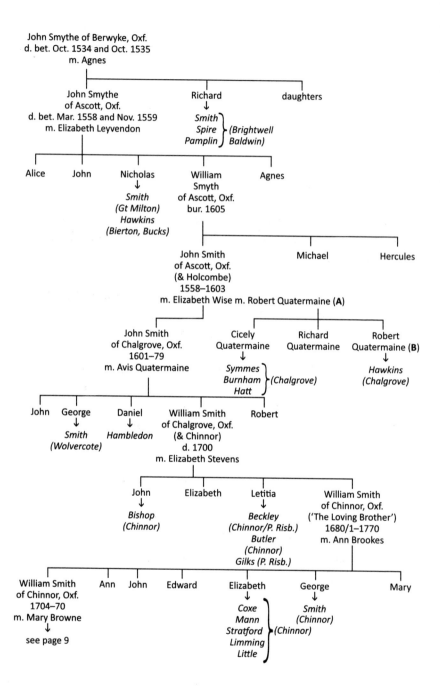

John Smythe of Berwyke, Oxf.
d. bet. Oct. 1534 and Oct. 1535
m. Agnes

John Smythe
of Ascott, Oxf.
d. bet. Mar. 1558 and Nov. 1559
m. Elizabeth Leyvendon

Richard
↓
Smith
Spire } *(Brightwell*
Pamplin } *Baldwin)*

daughters

Alice   John   Nicholas
↓
Smith
(Gt Milton)
Hawkins
(Bierton, Bucks)

William
Smyth
of Ascott, Oxf.
bur. 1605

Agnes

John Smith
of Ascott, Oxf.
(& Holcombe)
1558–1603
m. Elizabeth Wise m. Robert Quatermaine (**A**)

Michael

Hercules

John Smith
of Chalgrove, Oxf.
1601–79
m. Avis Quatermaine

Cicely
Quatermaine
↓
Symmes
Burnham } *(Chalgrove)*
Hatt

Richard
Quatermaine

Robert
Quatermaine (**B**)
↓
Hawkins
(Chalgrove)

John   George
↓
Smith
(Wolvercote)

Daniel
↓
Hambledon

William Smith
of Chalgrove, Oxf.
(& Chinnor)
d. 1700
m. Elizabeth Stevens

Robert

John
↓
Bishop
(Chinnor)

Elizabeth

Letitia
↓
Beckley
(Chinnor/P. Risb.)
Butler
(Chinnor)
Gilks (P. Risb.)

William Smith
of Chinnor, Oxf.
('The Loving Brother')
1680/1–1770
m. Ann Brookes

William Smith
of Chinnor, Oxf.
1704–70
m. Mary Browne
↓
see page 9

Ann   John   Edward   Elizabeth
↓
Coxe
Mann
Stratford } *(Chinnor)*
Limming
Little

George
↓
Smith
(Chinnor)

Mary

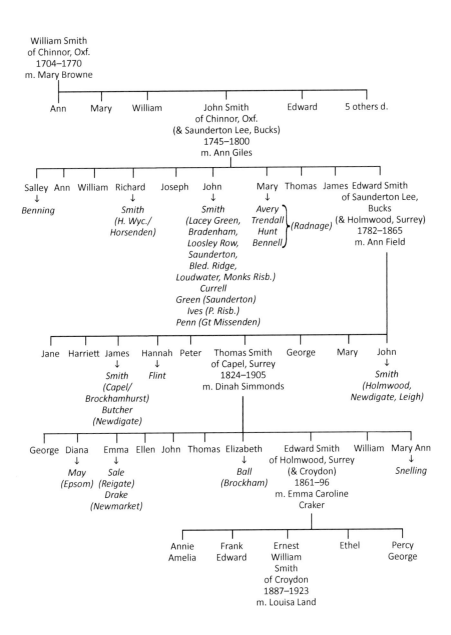

William Smith
of Chinnor, Oxf.
1704–1770
m. Mary Browne

Ann   Mary   William   John Smith   Edward   5 others d.
of Chinnor, Oxf.
(& Saunderton Lee, Bucks)
1745–1800
m. Ann Giles

Salley   Ann   William   Richard   Joseph   John   Mary   Thomas   James   Edward Smith
↓   ↓   ↓   ↓   of Saunderton Lee,
Benning   *Smith*   *Smith* *Avery*   Bucks
                          (H. Wyc./   *(Lacey Green,* *Trendall* *(Radnage)* (& Holmwood, Surrey)
                          Horsenden)   *Bradenham,* *Hunt*   1782–1865
                                                 Loosley Row, *Bennell*   m. Ann Field
                                                 Saunderton,
                                                 Bled. Ridge,
                                                 Loudwater, Monks Risb.)
                                                 Currell
                                                 Green (Saunderton)
                                                 Ives (P. Risb.)
                                                 Penn (Gt Missenden)

Jane   Harriett   James   Hannah   Peter   Thomas Smith   George   Mary   John
                    ↓   ↓   of Capel, Surrey   ↓
                 Smith   *Flint*   1824–1905   *Smith*
                 (Capel/   m. Dinah Simmonds   *(Holmwood,*
                 Brockhamhurst)   *Newdigate, Leigh)*
                 Butcher
                 (Newdigate)

George   Diana   Emma   Ellen   John   Thomas   Elizabeth   Edward Smith   William   Mary Ann
          ↓   ↓   ↓   of Holmwood, Surrey   ↓
        May   *Sale*   *Ball*   (& Croydon)   *Snelling*
        (Epsom) *(Reigate)*   *(Brockham)*   1861–96
                 Drake   m. Emma Caroline
                 (Newmarket)   Craker

                                   Annie   Frank   Ernest   Ethel   Percy
                                   Amelia   Edward   William   George
                                                     Smith
                                                     of Croydon
                                                     1887–1923
                                                     m. Louisa Land

Eltham Church and the war memorial upon which the name of Ernest William Smith is commemorated.

I. F. SMALL
E. W. SMITH
I. M. S. SMITH
S. W. SMITH
W. F. SMITH
C. P. SPARKES

1

'Their Name Liveth For Evermore'

E. W. SMITH – the moment I read the name carved in stone, something stirred within me. It was a Friday evening. Daddy and I were on our way to the cinema, as usual, but for some reason he had taken me across to the War Memorial, set in the church wall, and had pointed out his Father's name. I have often wondered why. For I was the sort of child about whom my Grandmother had once said, 'Where did you get <u>that</u> one!?' and yet from that very first moment, my Grandad became special to me and, child though I was, I somehow felt that I <u>had</u> to know more about him. Daddy knew only that his Father had been gassed during the 1914–18 War and had died when he was just seven years of age, which must have been why he had never spoken of him. In fact, now that I came to think of it, no-one had ever mentioned him.

So who could I ask? Not Grandma. She lived in Devon, which was right across the other side of the country, and although we would see her in the summer, I could not possibly wait that long! I had to know now!

My search for something more unearthed a large sepia photograph, hidden away in the shed, which I later discovered had once hung above Grandma's dining table, surrounded by silk poppies, but my excitement turned to disappointment when I saw that it was the same as one of the two smaller ones kept in the drawer of the sideboard. At least I knew what he looked like, but otherwise, that, it seemed, was that. My many questions had remained unanswered. The old family papers which I had looked through, much to my Mother's consternation, had yielded nothing. Grandad Smith was shrouded in mystery – and was to remain so, until another century, still more than forty years away, had finally dawned .....

1980 was, however, a most significant year. Forced to move to Bristol, I was desperately homesick and in need of something to occupy my mind, other than the remote possibility of moving back to Kent. The BBC television series 'Family History', presented by the newsreader Gordon Honeycombe, thus came at exactly the right time and I found it ABSOLUTELY FASCINATING! Each eagerly-awaited programme provided me with useful information which I jotted down in a notebook, and further notebooks were filled with still more information gleaned from the book which accompanied the series entitled *Discovering Your Family History*' by Don Steel, and from the many others on every aspect of family history, which were beginning to line my bookshelves.

Sadly, my Father had died at an early age, within a few short years of taking me across to the War Memorial, and as my Mother was therefore living alone and we were so far away, she spent every alternate three weeks with us. This enabled me to question her at great length, about anything and everything, and as she liked nothing better than to talk about the past, the pages of yet another notebook were quickly covered with her recollections. I was later to realise the importance of this, as even the most seemingly insignificant things were to prove useful.

To begin with, my husband was my researcher. For although he had no interest in family history, he so wanted me to settle in Bristol that he offered to visit the General Register Office at St Catherine's House to search the indexes for birth, marriage and death certificates and/or the Public Record Office in Chancery Lane to look through any available censuses on microfiche and obtain prints, whenever he was in London and oh, how I looked forward to those visits! I prepared for them weeks in advance, but then it always seemed such a long time to wait. Each branch of the family had a different coloured file, in the front of which was a page entitled 'Next Moves' which I kept updated. In the weeks leading up to a visit to London, I referred to those lists, filled out the appropriate search forms and placed them in order – those which would provide the most information first. Needless to say, the name on the first few was always Ernest William Smith. For that feeling that I <u>must</u> find out about him had stirred again – and how! He was the star that I reached for – the jewel in the crown. But with so little to help me, was it just a dream that might never come true?

The Devon and Cornwall branches of the family were soon back to the start of registration and, as we lived near enough to visit the County Record Offices and thus search the parish registers for baptisms, marriages and burials, reached steadily back into the 16th and 17th centuries. But of Grandad Smith I could find no trace. I waited and waited, at first for my husband to go to London and then for him to return, hoping that perhaps this time I had come up with the reason why we had not found the entry in the index before, but as soon as the waiting was over, my hopes were dashed yet again.

Then at last came the moment of breakthrough! Or so I thought. I had found a reference for the marriage certificate, which had to be right, and my excitement knew no bounds. For the marriage had taken place in Tiverton, just as I had been told, and my Land research had shown that Grandma was the only Louisa Land in Tiverton at that time. It seemed hard to believe that, after all these years, I would soon know who my Grandad was, yet the certificate arrived and it <u>was</u> right. There was Grandma, aged twenty-three, the daughter of Walter Land, <u>BUT</u> in that same column, where the name of Grandad's father should have been given, there was a dash! It was that upon which I was <u>so</u> relying, thus I need not try to describe how I felt. Illegitimacy was of course my first thought and it was many years before it occurred to me that there could have been some other explanation. But what did it matter what the explanation was? It made no difference. I was back to square one again.

'Put on your thinking cap' my junior school teachers used to say and even as I held the certificate in my hand, that was what I did. Consequently, off went a letter to the Ministry of Defence, requesting a copy of Grandad's Army Service Record. Those of Grandad Brett and Great-Grandad Brooks, who were of an earlier period and whose records were thus at the Public Record Office at Kew (now The National Archives), had yielded a wealth of information and I would have been content with just something! But I could fill out so few of the boxes on the form and, as I have since been told by Ronald Clifton, the Historical Advisor of the Western Front Association, *'To look for a man by the name of Smith in the Royal Artillery is the highest mountain that anyone can ever hope to climb'*. Thus back came the long-awaited reply, with regrets that the papers of Ernest William Smith must have been amongst those destroyed by enemy action during the Blitz. Yet another door had slammed in my face.

Undaunted – or at least that was what I told myself – I doubled my efforts at St Catherine's House. The one piece of concrete evidence that I had, was that he had died when my Father was seven, which meant that I was looking for a death certificate around 1923–24. That in itself was a problem though, for as the Commonwealth War Graves records come to an end at December 1921, no help could be gleaned from that source. A Sergeant or otherwise a Quartermaster Sergeant serving with the Royal Field Artillery and living, as we thought, in married quarters in Woolwich, he should have been registered somewhere in that area. It was also said that, when gassed, he had been a patient at the Royal Herbert Hospital there. Moreover, my Father had grown up on the outskirts of Eltham, but a stone's throw from the garrison town. That period had been checked over and over again though, and there was no Ernest William Smith anywhere near Woolwich. The only death recorded in the vicinity of London at that time was one in Colindale about a month before Daddy's seventh birthday ..... I had never even heard of the place and only sent for the certificate as a last resort for, if nothing else, at least I could rule that one out. When the certificate arrived, however, in the column headed 'Informant' was the name of my Grandmother and her address was given as Brookhill Married Quarters, Woolwich! I could hardly believe it. Apparently Grandad had been an Army pensioner and had died on 20th March 1923 at Colindale Hospital in North London. Presumably he must have been sent to the Royal Herbert Hospital to start with and then, as the gas continued to eat away at his lungs, had been moved to Colindale, which may have been an isolation hospital. Most importantly though, I had found him and now felt sure that I would be able to trace his birth. For I envisaged all the much-needed information turning up amongst the hospital records, but my enquiries, via another nearby hospital in the absence of a telephone number for Colindale, resulted only in the dampening news that the Colindale Hospital had closed in recent years and that no records had survived.

The euphoria which I had felt at finally having found something was but fleeting. There was nothing much to be gleaned from that certificate, other than Grandad's age, which was in agreement with that given at the time of his marriage. That was, of course, the age which my Grandmother would have been going by when registering his death, but it could not have been right. For I had been told that he was from Croydon and there were no Ernest William Smith births registered in Croydon in 1888! And if he came from anywhere else, I hadn't a hope!

It was then that I thought of my Aunt in Devon. The eldest of the children, she had been close to her mother and had always taken an interest in family matters. If anyone

Ernest William Smith.

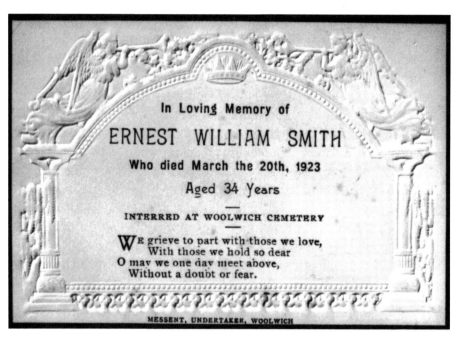

Burial card which Reg, son of Ernest, discovered amongst his possessions long after the burial entry was found.

knew anything about Grandad, <u>she</u> would. I broached the subject over a cup of tea and a slice of home-made cake and, amid interruptions from my youngest child, the facts began to emerge. He had had *'beautiful hands'* .... was very strict .... had had a temper .... was proud of the way that he had worked his way up in his Army career *'because of his sums'*.... he had set work for the children whenever he took Grandma out in the evenings and had sat up to mark it when they came home .... Into my ever-open notebook went all of this, together with one or two places where he had been stationed during and after the war. Whatever was known of him, however insignificant it might seem, I wanted to know. It was like piecing together another photograph and I hung on every word. The children demanded attention, however, there were other things to talk about and the clock marched on. Thus it was just as we were about to leave that I hurriedly began to ask pointed questions and, as we drove away, the most important facts were going round and round in my head – a sister called Annie .... two brothers .... one a Sergeant Major and one who drove a tram .... family *'up north'* .... and that upon which I was pinning my hopes .... his birthday was in July! Now I would find him, I felt sure.

Yet again though, my confidence was misplaced. I had not allowed for the fact that the name 'Annie' was fashionable in Victorian times. There were so many Annie Smiths, that I hadn't a hope of discovering which of them was ours. Nothing had changed. There were still no births of an Ernest William Smith in 1888 and that was a stumbling-block which I could not overcome. The age that he had given at the time of his marriage must have been wrong. There was no other explanation. It occurred to me that women are notorious for taking a few years off of their age, but that men might perhaps add a few years on, if the love of their life happened to be just that little bit older, as so many had when too young to join the Army and fight in the war. The search was therefore extended, which was how I came across an Ernest William Smith born in Croydon in the December quarter of 1890. The elation I felt, however, was dampened by the fact that a July birth should have been registered in the September quarter and it therefore came as no surprise to find that when the certificate arrived, the date of birth was in October. I tried to tell myself that the wrong date may have been given in order to avoid paying a fine – I had read that somewhere – but I did not really believe that, and that certificate somehow took away all my hope. How would I ever know for certain whether it was right? I had no proof. I was clutching at straws. Unless there was something somewhere which undoubtedly referred to my Grandad and contained some clue to his past, I could never be entirely sure, and thus with a heavy heart I filed the certificate away and with it my hopes of ever finding my Grandad.

2

800 Ernests!

Back in Kent at last, after more than twenty-five years in the West Country, we had finally finished the unpacking and most of the decorating and were gradually finding time for more pleasant pursuits. Thus, almost five years into the new century, I sat down to study a Christmas present received at a time when my mind was filled with the imminence of the move and which had therefore lain untouched, in amongst other unsorted papers, until the trauma was over and things were settled. Although it looked like just a piece of paper, it was, in fact, a chink of light in a long, dark tunnel. For there, in the 1901 Census index, were all of the Ernest Smiths born in Croydon, aged between seven and fifteen years (explanation as to why later) and the moment I looked through them, that long-ago feeling overwhelmed me. Grandad <u>had</u> to be one of those Ernests and now he was moving with the times! For my computer-literate daughter, Angela, having grown up hearing the name of Grandad Smith and seeing him gazing down at her from the wall, had printed the list as a surprise present and was encouraging me to try again – this time with her help. She was as intent on finding out who he was as I was and soon became the driving-force behind me.

Our first step was to print the households of any Ernests who were living in Croydon, but none looked hopeful. There was not one with a sister called Annie and two brothers. I therefore began to question whether it was my father or my mother who had told me that his father came from Croydon. So many years had passed, that I could not remember and that was all-important. For if it was my mother, she could have been in a muddle, as both my father and his brother were born there and, in any case, I had been told that Grandad came from Croydon. I did not know for certain that he was born there. Perhaps he had moved there after the age of three and would not therefore have been in the 1891 Census, but surely he ought to have been there by the age of thirteen, and thus in the 1901 Census, or that would not have been said of him. This was certainly a possibility. A list of Ernests born anywhere in the country and living in Croydon was therefore our next step, but none of their households afforded us even a glimmer of hope.

I would like to say that we were undaunted, but when faced with more than 800 Ernest Smiths born anywhere in the country and living anywhere in the country – even Wales! – we were somewhat downhearted, to say the least! But then, now that doubt had been cast upon whether he had come from Croydon, we could not even be sure that he had been there as a young child and he could therefore have been anywhere! My daughter's argument, however, was that he must have had family there by the 1914–18 War, or he would not have taken his young wife and their new baby away from her family in Devon to a place which was to suffer Zeppelin raids. Admittedly he was able to visit her there whilst training in the Midlands, but why not take her to the Midlands? That would have made more sense and he must therefore have had a reason for taking her to Croydon.

By this time, we had, of course, been trying to find Annie, but, as I said before, that proved to be an even more popular name than Ernest and, to make matters worse, the enumerator could have written it down as Ann! None of the Annies born in Croydon and/or living in Croydon tied up with any of the Ernests and, depending upon her age, she could perhaps have gone into service by 1901 and might therefore have been living in some other household – again anywhere!

The 800 Ernests were therefore our only hope and Angela had had an idea. For although the 1901 Census index showed only the first Christian name, if another name or initial had been given and was in the enumerator's pages, this information was stored and could be used to sort the data. We therefore asked the computer for all Ernest William Smiths aged seven to fifteen; followed by Ernest W. Smiths aged seven to fifteen. Of course, the printouts received were identical to those in our original list of 800 Ernests in that they showed only the first name, but we now knew that those were in fact Ernest Williams or Ernest Ws and the original printouts were therefore marked accordingly. Not that that meant that Grandad was one of them. Indeed none seemed at all likely, which was why we had to try to whittle down the remaining Ernests still further, as although he had had a second Christian name, depending upon the information given to the enumerator, he could have been listed as simply Ernest. Our next step was, therefore, to ask for all Ernest A. Smiths aged seven to fifteen; followed by Ernest B. Smiths, Ernest C. Smiths, etc., etc., working our way through the alphabet. After that we tried to think of every possible male Christian name from that period and asked for all Ernest Albert Smiths, all Ernest Algernon Smiths, all Ernest Bernard Smiths, all Ernest Charles Smiths, etc., etc. Again the printouts showed only the name of Ernest, but we matched them to the original ones in our list of 800 Ernests and were able to cross those off, as they could not be Grandad. By this means, we managed to whittle the list down to about 600. So what next?

We thought and thought and came up with the fact that he was a bachelor when he married. Perhaps that might help, as any of the 600 who had married before he had, (October 1913), could be ruled out. It would have been much too expensive to obtain the certificates for all Ernest Smith marriages between 1901 and October 1913, but we hoped to correlate each one of the Ernests in the 1901 Census index with a birth entry and marriage entry in the same registration districts in the General Register Office indexes, in order to eliminate that Ernest. Now, in accordance with this, we acquired the birth entries from the Online General Register Office indexes for any Ernest Smiths in the country from 1885 – March 1894. The two photographs, taken within a year of the marriage, or four at the most, had been studied more carefully prior to this and it had been decided that Grandad could not have been under twenty when he married, even allowing for the fact that people tended to look older than their years at that time. This was why we had printed the Ernests from age seven (born 1893/4) in the 1901 Census and, similarly, having been said to have been in his early thirties when he died, he could not have been more than thirty-seven at that time, hence the ones aged fifteen (born 1885/6). We had of course to also obtain the death entries from 1885, (the date of the earliest birth), as we had to take these into account. A much longer period had to be covered for these entries in order to improve our chances of whittling down the numbers still more, as although Grandad died in his thirties, one of the others could have lived to be well over ninety, (fortunately the death index includes the age from 1866). Ernest William, son of James and Elizabeth Smith, born in Croydon in October 1890, whose certificate I had had filed away for more than twenty years, was now found to have died before his first birthday, poor little chap, as had another born in Croydon in the March quarter of 1894, but we now had one who was beginning to look hopeful .... born in Croydon in 1887 – in the September quarter – which could have meant a July birthday – he did not seem to be amongst the marriages, nor amongst the deaths. Although, strangely enough, neither was he in the 1901 Census ....

Whether our attempt to eliminate some of the 600 Ernests by using the General Register Office indexes would have achieved the required results, we shall never know. For whilst whittling them down still more, we were also exploring every avenue, in the hope that someone somewhere might come up with a clue. Which was why I telephoned the Tiverton Registry Office, where my Grandparents were married, to ask about the procedure at that time. I was fortunate enough to speak to a very helpful lady, who explained that couples were asked to fill out a form, which was put on display for three weeks, and the marriage certificate was completed in accordance with the details shown thereon. This gave us something to think about. For it was not as if he had been asked outright, *'What is the name and occupation of your father?'* and if his father had died when he was a child, perhaps he had not thought it necessary to fill out those two boxes. The omission would not have been questioned. To have done so would have been indelicate (if he was illegitimate). Or perhaps he had not known his father's Christian name. That may seem strange to us in our free and easy, first-name-orientated society, but Victorian times were very much stricter and much more conventional and a man was unlikely to have been addressed as anything other than *'Mr Smith'* by his neighbours, or by anyone whom he was likely to have met in the street. Moreover, often even a husband and wife would have addressed each other as *'Mr'* or *'Mrs'* in front of the children. We therefore tried to put ourselves in Grandad's place. There he was, right across the other side of the country from his family, about to get married. He had asked for Louisa's hand and they had set the date, when he was suddenly confronted by such a form. What was he to do? Ask her to wait, whilst he wrote to his mother or sister to ask for the information; that is if in fact they could read and write, which was not all that likely, inasmuch as schooling had only recently become compulsory? A proud man, so we have been told, he was more likely to have just omitted to fill out those two boxes and got on with making her his wife!

The helpful lady in the Tiverton Registry Office also gave me some very useful advice. Apparently, those in the Registrars' Offices will not give out information, but they will <u>confirm</u> something if given information. Thus when I told her that Grandad was born in July, she said that if I telephoned any of the Registrar's Offices to ask about an entry in the General Register Office indexes and merely said, *'Was this Ernest William Smith who was registered in the September quarter of, for example, 1887, born in July?'* they would answer, *'Yes'* or *'No'* free of charge. Then, if I wanted any further details, I would have to write in and pay the fee. Consequently, that was exactly what I did, beginning with the hopeful Ernest in Croydon and <u>yes! He was born in July</u>!!!! Others as far and wide as Swansea, King's Lynn and Stockton-on-Tees were queried. Some of them were also born in July, others were able to be discarded. Some Registrars' Offices were most helpful, others insisted that I wrote in, but promised to refund the fee if the Ernest in question was not born in July.

As previously mentioned, we were exploring every avenue, and therefore in the hope of finding Grandad's Army Service Record at The National Archives or of finding him in the Medal Rolls, Angela spent a day there. This was, however, a long and completely fruitless day, at the end of which, because she had found absolutely nothing and had only ten minutes until closing time, she decided to look for an Ernest William Smith in Croydon in the 1891 Census before leaving. And only one came up .... aged three, he was the son of Edward and Emma Caroline, the youngest of three children, the others being Frank Edward and <u>ANNIE</u> Amelia!!! Admittedly there was only one brother, but his parents were young enough to have had more children in years to come. With bated breath, we searched our 1901 Census pages for him, but he simply was not there! Nor, it seemed, were any of the rest of the family. For although there were many Edward, Emma and Frank Smiths in Croydon, none were the right age, and as the columns headed 'Administrative County' did not match, presumably they were not living in the same household. We fared better with the Annies, in that there were more possibilities, although upon checking the households, we found that none were the right one.

On looking at a street map of Croydon, we saw that Gloucester Road, where Edward and Emma Caroline's family were living in the 1891 Census, was only just around the corner from where my father was born, which was where Grandad had taken Grandma during the 1914–18 War! Excited by this, we sent for the certificate of 'the hopeful Ernest' – the Ernest William Smith born in Croydon in the September quarter of 1887 – hoping that <u>he</u> was <u>their</u> son, and when we saw that he was, we were elated. However, our feelings upon receiving the certificate are best described as 'wistful'. Was he our Grandad? If only we knew .... neither Angela nor I would have just wanted someone who fitted the bill. It was no good picking out an Ernest with a nice family in the right sort of place. He had to be <u>ours</u> – our Grandad, who had always been so special to me and had become so to her. This one seemed so right, but was he?

Although we thought it unlikely that my Uncle Reg, the youngest of Grandad's children, born in 1918, would remember any more than my father, that said, Jack had married at the early age of twenty, whereas Reg had remained at home with his mother for another twelve years and even after marriage, for a while. In the hope, therefore, that during that time something may have been said that might be of use, I wrote to him. Though nearly ninety, he did his best to remember and did in fact come up with two snippets of information which I had not heard before. Firstly, that his father's father was a builder, or something of the sort, and, secondly, he had but a faint recollection that there had been some mention of *'a boy soldier'* - Grandad perhaps? – *'put in the Army by his mother'*. Any record of such an early Army career would, we were told, have been with his Army Service Record, wherever that was, so no help was to be gleaned from that, but it was the words *'by his <u>mother</u>'* which interested us. For in Victorian and Edwardian times, that was something which a man would have done rather than a woman – unless she was a widow who had fallen on hard times .... and if Grandad's mother <u>was</u> a widow and his father had thus died when he was a child, that, as we have said before, could have accounted for the fact that he perhaps did not know his Christian name .... The computer was therefore asked for lists of all Smith builders, and all Smith widows living in Croydon in the 1901 Census and amongst the widows was an Emma with a fifteen year old son called Ernest and another son, Percy, aged seven. She was aged thirty-two, whereas the Emma Caroline in the 1891 Census (wife of Edward) would have been thirty-six, and Edward and Emma Caroline's son, Ernest, would only have been thirteen. But was Percy the other brother ....?

Some of the builders' households and those of the other widows were viewed, but nothing came of this. We still had only the one hopeful Ernest, the Ernest William Smith, son of Edward and Emma Caroline in the 1891 Census, and even he had disappeared. No marriage or death entries which matched him could be found in the General Register Office indexes before 1913, yet nor was he in the 1901 Census. Unless of course the ages were wrong and he was the son of Emma, the widow (if Edward had died).

We therefore searched for any Edward Smith deaths between 1891 and 1901 and the computer came up with two possible entries: Edward Smith aged twenty-nine in the March quarter of 1892 and Edward Smith aged thirty-three in the September quarter of 1896. The ages disagreed with that given in the 1891 Census, but it is often the case that the age shown on a death certificate is incorrect, as someone other than the person themself is giving the information.

We were easily able to rule out one of these possibilities by searching the General Register Office indexes for the birth of a Percy Smith about 1893/4. For, as the earliest one was in the September quarter of 1893, the Edward who had died in the March quarter of 1892 could not have been the father of any of the three found. Consequently, if the Emma in the 1901 census was the widow of an Edward, it had to be the one who had died in the September quarter of 1896.

The Ernest in the aforementioned family was, however, only 'hopeful'. We had no definite proof that he was our Grandad, which was why I now started writing to everyone that I could think of who might be able to help. I had, of course, applied yet again to the Army Personnel Centre in Glasgow for Grandad's Service Record and the completed form, payment and written permission from my uncle, who was his next-of-kin, had been returned to them. There was, however, a long wait ahead and during that time, I took advantage of the list of contacts which they had sent and wrote to the Veterans' Agency.

I knew for certain that Grandad had received a pension, as it had stopped when he died and Grandma had had a struggle to make ends meet. We had grown so accustomed to receiving negative replies though, that it came as some surprise when photocopies arrived of two index cards and a page from a book. The date of death and address matched those on Grandad's death certificate. Grandma's name was shown but, best of all, two service numbers were given! This was our first real clue and with a name like Smith the importance of a service number cannot be understated. I studied every single letter shown on those photocopies, in case I had missed something, and having noticed a Chelsea Number, telephoned The National Archives to query it. I was referred to the Chelsea Hospital and my hopes soared. The records were sure to include a date of birth and already I was building castles in the air. But I had not allowed for the fact that as Grandad had died in the 1920s, his papers had been put with his Army Service Record and were, supposedly, at the Army Personnel Centre....

By July, the month in which Grandad was born, we were no further forward, but were cheered by the thought of placing some flowers on his grave and I therefore wrote to Eltham Church to ask where it was. For, as his name was commemorated on the War Memorial set in the church wall, I had foolishly assumed that he was buried there and had never bothered to ask my mother if it was indeed so. Yet she must have known, as she had often said that, at Daddy's request, she had placed her wedding bouquet of dark red carnations, (chosen especially as they were Grandad's favourite flower), on his father's grave after the ceremony. Where that grave was though, we might never know and I had only myself to blame.

The letter before me stated that there was no Ernest William Smith in the card index of grave numbers and enclosed was a photocopy of a page of burials, both before and after Grandad's date of death, as further proof. We were advised to try the Cemeteries Department, but having looked at a street map of Woolwich and found a church near to Brookhill Married Quarters, where the family were living, sent a postal enquiry instead to the London Metropolitan Archives, where the records are held. Again, it was a negative response – the churchyard was full by the 1920s – and again we were referred to the Cemeteries Department.

A telephone call to the relevant office yielded nothing however. No burial of an Ernest William Smith could be found at that time, in any of the cemeteries in either the Eltham or Woolwich area! Had Grandma been unable to afford to bring him back from Colindale? She had, after all, had a struggle to make ends meet. Yet I found it hard to believe that my mother had travelled by train all the way to North London, to place her wedding bouquet there, without having made some mention of the fact when recalling the occasion. A further telephone call, this time to Firepower,

The Royal Artillery Museum, assured me that the Army would have covered the cost of Grandad returning home and I then felt sure that there had been an oversight. For, yet again, we had studied the street map and had found a cemetery only a short distance from the married quarters. The young man at the Cemeteries Department, who in answer to my subsequent telephone call instigated a further search, inspired confidence and rightly so. Although I doubt if he has ever met with a response which can equal that which followed his eventual discovery of Grandad's grave in Woolwich New Cemetery!

The path we trod in search of it had changed so little that it was easy to envisage a young widow and her children in their hour of grief. But now when we look along that path, we see an array of silk poppies and beyond them a fine, new stone, where once there was an unmarked grave.

Long before that was in place though, we had set to work again, penning letters to every possible source, both tried and untried. Would the Electoral Rolls for Tiverton from 1908–1916 (the date of my father's birth in Croydon) throw any light upon how my Grandparents, from opposite sides of the country, had met and thus on Grandad's life prior to the 1914–18 War? Unfortunately the reply from the Devon Record Office told only of my Great-Grandfather, Walter Land, at the address given. Had the General Register Office entries for the September quarter 1888 perhaps gone astray? I had read that this sometimes happened, but that the Local Registrar kept copies. If only .... But the reply to the letter to the Croydon Registrar's Office confirmed that that was not the case. A negative reply came also from the Greenwich Heritage Centre. There was no obituary in either of the local newspapers, nor was Grandad in the Electoral Roll there. Another faint hope lay in the fact that Grandma's parents were Salvationists and letters were sent to the Salvation Army in both Croydon and Tiverton, in case she had met Ernest William Smith through that means, but yet again no trace was found of him amongst their records. He was known to have worked for the Pearl Assurance Company, but their records had not survived. The librarian at Colchester Library was most helpful and an Ernest William Smith with a wife called Louisa, was actually found in the Electoral Roll in the early 1920s, when Grandad was said to have been stationed there. But although he disappeared from the list of names, she was still listed in the 1930s, long after Grandma was known to have been living in Eltham, so unless a mistake had been made, it cannot have been them. (What a cruel coincidence that one of the 800 Ernests had married a Louisa and was living in the right place at the right time!) Finally yet another letter was sent to Firepower, The Royal Artillery Museum. I had written to Paul Evans, the Librarian there, before but now that we had the service numbers, we were more hopeful.

A busy man though, Paul had not yet replied and thus it was that we set off for the Croydon Local Studies Library still none the wiser and somewhat downhearted. At the back of my mind though, were my Aunt's words, *'He was proud of how he had worked his way up because of his sums.'* Grandad must therefore have gone to school and I felt sure that if he was anywhere, he would be in the schools records – as long as they had survived!

I had the feeling that in Croydon, the place that Grandad must have loved, as he took his family there during wartime, we would find something and we were fortunate in that the Archivist, Chris Bennett, was most helpful. The Local Studies Library, though small, was packed with sources of information, which included an excellent collection of schools admission registers and logbooks; large-scale street maps; old photographs; a set of street directories covering the period 1849–1939; and newspapers on microfilm, to name but a few, and as we had decided to begin with the admission registers, the large, leather-bound volumes from 1890–1910 were brought to us, two at a time. The nearest school to the road in which my father was born and to that in which Edward and Emma Caroline and their family were living in the 1891 Census, was Sydenham Road Junior Boys, which therefore seemed like a good place to start. An index at the front of the book enabled us to see at a glance that already we had stumbled across an Ernest W. Smith, and by using the reference number, 1676, beside his name to locate the full entry, we found that he was another Ernest William. We thought at first that he was the son of the aforementioned family, as his father was shown as Edward Smith, but his date of birth was 13th July 1886, whereas their son was born on 23rd July 1887. Could this have been a mistake? We had hoped to check it in the Senior Boys' register, but this Ernest had transferred to another school in 1897, one of the few which had retained its registers.

The search for Ernest Smiths continued and nine were found in all, some with second Christian names, others who were just Ernest. Each one was noted down, along with his date of birth, address and parentage, for future reference. For the parent may have omitted to give a second Christian name, which could have been William, or alternatively, an Ernest Charles may later have been found in a street directory or some other such source, listed simply as Ernest and we would then need to know that he was in fact Ernest Charles and not another contender. Of those nine, five were ruled out as either too old, or because of having a second Christian name, and of the four with whom we were left, one was found in the census with <u>four</u> brothers and <u>two</u> sisters and therefore seemed most unlikely. That left three, to which were added two more Ernests, whose families had been found in the printed copy of the 1891 Census, kept at the Croydon Local Studies Library. Harry E. Smith and his wife, Mary, had a son Ernest, aged three and an unnamed daughter, aged 0, whom we thought might turn out to be Annie. This Ernest was born in London and had not therefore featured in those 'born in Croydon' in the 1901 Census or, as far as we could tell, in those born elsewhere. The other Ernest, also aged three, was the son of Mary Ann.

He had two brothers and she may have had a daughter at a later date. Both were therefore possibilities.

There was, however, only one who was known to be an Ernest William – the son of Edward, in the Sydenham Road School admissions register – and, as we had not come across him in any other registers, the Archivist suggested that we should contact Woodside, the school to which he had transferred. The location was pointed out to us on the large-scale map and when we set about looking for the school later in the day, we were surprised to find how near it was to the streets with which we had become familiar. For the preceding hours had been spent following Edward and Emma Caroline, the parents of the Ernest William Smith in the 1891 Census, from one to another, by referring to the local street directories. We began by looking at 185 Gloucester Road, his place of birth, in 1887, the year of his birth and the occupier/head of the house was listed as *'Edward Smith'*. The next year was taken down from the shelf, and the next, and again, the name of the occupier/head of the house was *'Edward Smith'*. In 1891 this changed to *'C. Lambourne'*, and we therefore looked at 92 Gloucester Road, the address given in the 1891 Census, and found Edward there. He was shown at this address until 1895, although as the Archivist had told us that the street directories were compiled at the end of the previous year, the family must have moved during 1895. Not knowing where to look in the next directory, we tried 1 Johnson Road, the address of the Ernest William Smith, son of Edward, in the Sydenham Road School admissions register, when he started school on 2nd July 1895, but the occupier was *'C. Craker'*. In the subsequent directories, 1897 – 1903, it was *'Robert Craker'*. The name of Craker was, however, familiar, as we knew from the 1887 birth certificate, that it was Emma Caroline's maiden name .... Did this mean that Ernest William, son of Edward and Emma Caroline and Ernest William, son of Edward in the Sydenham Road School admissions register, were one and the same and that the date of birth in the register was therefore wrong and, if so, were they living with her family at that time? The reason for this may have been that Edward was ill and thus unable to work, as the 1895 entry at 92 Gloucester Road was the last mention of '*Edward Smith*', other than one in a completely different area, whom we jotted down just in case. This would then comply with the fact that there was a General Register Office death entry for an Edward Smith in the September quarter of 1896. Was this then Emma Caroline's Edward, and was she the Emma, widow, aged thirty-two, with the sons Ernest and Percy, in the 1901 Census? It certainly seemed probable, although we had to allow for the fact that they could have moved away and therefore continued to look for him in the nearby streets. A '*Mrs Smith, Laundress*' was found at 44 Cross Road and that was the occupation of Emma Caroline in the 1891 Census, but as Smith is such a common name, we could not be certain that it was her. We followed her from one address to another, wondering if it was because of her straitened circumstances that she moved so frequently, and came at length to 40 Edward Road in 1900–1902 .... the address of Emma, the widow in the 1901 Census, whose occupation was also laundress. Did this mean that she was Emma Caroline, the wife of Edward, and was her fifteen-year-old son the Ernest in the 1891 Census, who should have been aged thirteen? If so, and our earlier supposition that that Ernest was the one in the Sydenham Road School admissions register was correct, there would only be one Ernest William Smith! But was there?

We were to leave there with these all-important questions still unanswered and with another which I was to put to Paul Evans, the Librarian at Firepower, The Royal Artillery Museum. For we had found a mention of Grandad in the Absent Voters Lists for Autumn 1918 and Spring 1919, the entries having read '*Ernest William Smith, 43 Limes Road, 45138 RFA Sgt. 5th Res. Bde. (T)*'.

'*5th Reserve Bde. (Terr.s) was a unit based in the UK*',

he said, in answer to my telephone call. *'Ernest would have been at a big army camp recovering from having been gassed and would, meanwhile, have been training men, seeing to the wounded passing through and doing all his usual duties. It would have been a big job that he was doing, especially if he was a mature soldier'*, the implication being that these sort of men were the backbone of the army, and once again I had cause to be grateful to him. He knew so much, explained it so well and always did his best to help me, even though I was a nuisance to him. He never said so, but I felt sure that I must be. I had written and telephoned so many times. Yet I <u>had</u> to keep trying and when, after the long months of waiting, the dreaded reply was received from the Army Personnel Centre, confirming that the Service Record could not be found and what little hope we had had was finally dashed, who else should we have turned to but the Gunners, whose badge our Grandad must have worn with pride?

Paul's last letter had read, *'I am sorry to say that there is little we can do to help'*, but I wrote again, telling him of the 800 Ernests and imploring him. I did not want to give up until certain that I was beaten and with his expert knowledge of army records and procedures, perhaps he could think of something which I had overlooked. He was my last resort.

The weeks passed. The dark days of another new year afforded us no hope that the search would ever come to anything. Perhaps I was thinking something of the sort, as I fastened my coat in readiness for my early morning walk and the post fell onto the mat. I was handed a letter and, glancing down at the Firepower crest, read, *'Newly released enlistment books delivered to the regimental archives in December 2005, from the now demolished Army Personnel Centre, Hayes, contain some of the information you are searching for.'* I should have recognised the service number in front of his name, but I was too busy thinking that it would be some other Ernest William Smith.

34

It always was. *'Enlisted Stratford .... February 1907 ....'* The words meant nothing. But I came to the place of birth and my heart stood still! <u>CROYDON</u> was jumping out at me from the page! Afraid to hope or even to breathe, I read on, as though my life depended upon it. *'.... aged 19 years and 7 months .... suggests a date of birth in <u>JULY 1887</u>*!!!'

It was as if Grandad was calling across the years. For the answers to the questions put to him by the Recruiting Officer, were those for which we were searching! There was more, but at such a moment, I could hardly see it, let alone take it in, my eyes were so full of tears. Almost a lifetime ago, I had been shown his name on the War Memorial and at last – at long, long last – I knew who he was ....

3

At Last!

Words cannot even begin to describe how I felt as I walked down the lane that morning and, even now, whenever I try to recall the moment that I read that letter, the emotions stir within me. It was like a dream come true. I could hardly believe it and just could not stop smiling. Attached to the letter were photocopies of two pages from an attestment book which, in addition to name, rank, service numbers, date and place of enlistment, character, dates of service in France and of discharge, showed Grandma's name and the date of their marriage, the full names of the children and their dates and places of birth, his age, to the month, and his place of birth. And Grandad – God bless him! – had not only put down Croydon, but <u>WEST</u> Croydon, where he had taken Grandma during the war! Both my father and uncle were shown as having also been born in West Croydon and we already knew that they were born in one of those streets through which we had followed Edward and Emma Caroline and where their son, Ernest William, was born in the very same month and year that Grandad had said that he was born. There could therefore be no doubt whatsoever that he was their son, but having waited so long for such a moment, I nevertheless wanted to check on every last detail, whereupon something theretofore puzzling suddenly became clear.

We went first to Croydon, (where else!?) to look for the marriage of Edward Smith and Emma Caroline Craker and it was soon found on the microfilm of the parish register, on Christmas Eve 1881. She was aged sixteen and he a twenty year old labourer, yet he had a fine signature which befitted someone who was accustomed to writing, and which seemed to suggest that Grandad may have inherited his aptitude for schoolwork from the Smith line.

Disappointed however, that we had been unable to look for the baptisms of their children at the Local Studies Library, as the microfilm did not cover that period, we set off for the Surrey History Centre at Woking almost at once. For having waited long enough already, we were anxious to find the entries in the parish register.

Ernest William was baptized on 18th September 1887 at St James' Church, Croydon, but, strangely enough, his date of birth, which was given as 23rd July 1887 on the birth certificate, was shown therein as 25th! The baptisms of Annie Amelia and Frank Edward were found in 1882 and 1884 and there was a daughter, Ethel, baptized and buried in 1891. Another son, Percy George, was baptized in 1893, thus we now knew that the Emma Smith, widow, in Edward Road in the 1901 Census, was indeed Emma Caroline and that her eldest son, Ernest, aged fifteen, was in fact aged thirteen. There were no baptisms for either Edward or Emma Caroline, nor was there one for an Ernest, son of an Edward, in July 1886 (the one in the Sydenham Road School admissions register). We had been looking out for this, that we might discover who he was, and as he had no baptism, this suggested that he was in fact the son of Edward and Emma Caroline as we had thought. A point in favour of this, was that Robert Craker was occupying 1 Johnson Road, the address given when this Ernest started school, and we now knew from the marriage entry that he was the father of Emma Caroline. Consequently, following this visit to the Surrey History Centre, I wrote to the Croydon Registrar's Office, requesting that they might check for the birth entry. Back came a letter telling us that it did not exist. There was no Ernest William Smith born in 1886!

Our next step was therefore to contact Woodside School, to which this Ernest had transferred in 1897. None of the other Ernests were in West Croydon, except for one who was born in 1893 and was still living in Northbrook Road long after Grandad had enlisted in the Royal Field Artillery. Nor were they born anywhere near the right time, but this one was an Ernest William and his date of birth was so near to that which Grandad had put down, that he had made us uneasy. We had to know who he was!

Thankfully, when the photocopy of the relevant page from the Woodside admission register turned up in the post, the mystery was solved. Ernest William, son of Edward, supposedly born on 13th July 1886, who had transferred from Sydenham Road School to Woodside School in 1897, was shown as the son of Emma, of Exeter Road, previous school Sydenham Road, born 16th July 1887! This proved that Edward had died by 1897, as we had thought, and Exeter Road was one of the addresses to which we had followed 'Mrs Smith, laundress/Mrs E. Smith' in the 1898 Croydon street directory (compiled at the end of 1897). The most important thing which was proved, however, was that there was only one Ernest William Smith! The Woodside School entry also told us that Ernest William had left 13th July 1900, the comment 'at work'. One cannot help but form the opinion, that whilst Emma may perhaps have been a pretty, little thing, she certainly had no head for figures! A different date was shown in the Sydenham Road and Woodside School admission registers, when baptizing her son and when registering his birth. Moreover, both her age and his are wrong in the 1901 Census, yet in 1891, when Edward would have provided the details, the ages were all correct. One wonders if their son ever really knew whether his birthday was the 13th, 16th, 23rd or 25th or in which year he was born! Fortunately though, she never wavered from July!

We had begun to feel an affinity with this family. We like to think that it was intuition, for by now we so wanted them to be ours. There was, however, one last search which we had to undertake, in order to be absolutely certain and because we were so close to claiming them and just one entry in over 100 years could have swept away all our hopes, it was to prove the most traumatic of all. Having telephoned in advance to make an appointment, we were shown to a seat in the Croydon Cemeteries Office and the first of the large tomes, covering the burials from 1887, was brought to us. The rest were ranged along the shelves in a nearby room, together with other books in which one could look up the reference number given in the burial entry, in order to find out the age and address of the person and of anyone else who was buried in the same grave. These details enabled one to identify someone, if, for example, one was looking for a John Brown aged forty, and a possible entry was found. The one in question may have turned out to be aged seventeen and buried with other members of his family, all at the same address.

No General Register Office death entry had been found for Ernest William, son of Edward and Emma Caroline Smith, but in case we had overlooked it, we had decided to check for a burial from birth to 100 years of age. Thus tense, for fear that we might find the dreaded entry, we turned each page, jotting down the names and references for any of his family, or rather for anyone who could have been one of his family. We had, of course, to make a note of any Emma Smiths, Annies, Franks and Percys and, most importantly, any Ernests, as well as any Emma Caroline Smiths, Ernest Williams, etc., in case only one name had been given by the informant. Consequently, the list was vast and each one had to be looked up in the reference books.

By this time we had the death certificate for the Edward Smith who had died 16th August 1896 and knew that he was the husband of Emma Caroline, as he was living at 44 Cross Road, the address at which we had found *'Mrs Smith, laundress'* in that year, and also because the two schools' admission registers showed that Edward Smith, husband of Emma, had died between July 1895 and September 1897.

Now, whilst looking up the entries in the reference books, we found the burial of Edward and thought it touching that although Emma must have been finding it hard to make ends meet, as this was long before widows received pensions, she managed to scrape together enough to buy the grave. There were some anxious moments when, hardly daring to breathe, we rushed from one room to the other and quickly turned the pages of the reference book. The worst of these was towards the end of what seemed like such a very long day. But when we left there, spent though we were, we felt only elation. For there was no entry for Ernest William Smith, son of Edward and Emma Caroline. He was our Grandad!

One of the first moves that we made upon receiving the letter from Firepower, was to telephone the Army Personnel Centre. For only weeks had passed since their Administrative Officer, Carol Morrison, had written to say that the service record of Ernest William Smith could not be found and now that we knew his date and place of birth, his parentage and date and place of enlistment, we hoped that that might make a difference, as some mention had been made of insufficient information. Hopeful on our behalf, she very kindly offered to instigate a further search, this time by hand rather than by computer, and whilst awaiting the results, I wrote to one of the experts at The National Archives, to ask for advice as to the probable whereabouts of the service record. For Grandad's army career had spanned three different periods – pre-war, 1914–18 war and post-war. A most helpful reply was received, explaining that all of the records should be together and should be held by the Army Personnel Centre, as the records of those discharged during the 1920s had not yet been handed over to The National Archives. However, it was pointed out that, if misfiled, as sometimes happened, they could have been anywhere and would not then come to light.

My second question was whether Grandad was likely to have enlisted at Stratford-upon-Avon or Stratford in East London and the latter was thought more probable, as there were many more recruiting offices in and around the London area, in places where men were less likely to find employment. This complied with advice received from Gordon Rae of the Stratford-upon-Avon branch of the Western Front Association, who confirmed that there was only one recruiting office there in 1907, that being for those wishing to join the Royal Warwickshire Regiment. Asked also whether Grandad could have enlisted in the Territorial Army, he said that that was not formed until 1908 and that the initials TA following Grandad's service number in the Absent Voters List must thus have applied to his latter service, when a reservist.

Ronald Clifton, the Historical Advisor of the Western Front Association, thought it likely that Grandad had met a recruiter in Croydon and had been directed to Stratford in East London, where the Royal Artillery were recruiting. There he would have been given a medical examination before being sent to the garrison town of Woolwich to begin his training. At that time, the narrow, cobbled streets in some parts of the town were flanked by high, Victorian brick walls and whenever the Royal Artillery came tearing past at such a rate that the horses' hooves drew sparks from the cobbles, children walking to or from school, would pin themselves to the wall in terror and remain there until the last of the gun-carriages had gone up the steep hill and over the common to the parade ground.

There may have been a reason why Ernest was keen to join the Royal Field Artillery, for we have recently discovered that his elder brother, Frank, who was missing from the 1901 Census, had enlisted as a boy soldier at the age of fifteen (it must have been Frank, rather than Ernest, to whom my Uncle Reg was referring when he spoke of a boy soldier, which shows that there is often a grain of truth in stories handed down) and, having fought in the Boer War from 1899–1902, Frank was serving with the Royal Field Artillery in India at the time that Ernest enlisted. He must therefore have become something of a hero to him and was perhaps the reason why he too chose the Royal Field Artillery. He would have been encouraged to do so by the Recruiting Sergeant, as he was said to have been a big man and his height and build would thus have been well-suited to manning the guns.

What action he saw may always remain a mystery though. For we heard by way of a telephone call that the further search for his service record at the Army Personnel Centre had yielded nothing. Whether it was amongst those destroyed in the Blitz, is somewhere in the pipeline between the Army Personnel Centre and The National Archives, now that the 1920s records are being transferred, or was withdrawn when he received a pension and was then misfiled at The National Archives, we may never know.

He should also have had a medal index card, as he served in France and Flanders, 1916–17 and the page from the attestation book states that his conduct was exemplary, but that too seems to have gone astray. We searched for it ourselves and wrote to one of the sources recommended by a fellow member of the Western Front Association, in the hope that someone well-versed in military research might have more luck, but it has not yet come to light. However, the original cards were rescued by the Western Front Association, when The National Archives were discarding them, after putting them onto the computer and some of the members are very kindly looking through them on our behalf in case the one for which we are searching has been misfiled.

Of course, one cannot help but wish that the information contained in the missing records was available to us. Yet the loss of it is by far outweighed by those precious pages from the attestation book, sent to us by Paul Evans of Firepower, and with his help, that of Ronald Clifton of the Western Front Association, and the researcher at Tiverton Museum, my Aunt's recollections, the official 'Returns of the Army' held at The National Archives and, more recently, the 1911 Census, we have been able to piece together the latter part of Grandad's life.

We now know that, having enlisted on 1st February

1907, he served as a Gunner with the Royal Field Artillery and after his initial training at Woolwich and a brief spell at Bulford Camp in Wiltshire, was stationed at Hillsea Barracks, Portsmouth from September 1907 to September 1909. 150th Battery, with which he served, then moved to Topsham Road Barracks, Exeter and whilst he was there, Louisa Land must have taken a train into the little country town, as she so often did, for before he moved on yet again, to Brighton, in September 1911, their courtship had begun. Letters were perhaps the means by which their romance blossomed. Cherished letters which may have led at length to a proposal during one of his weekend visits to the family home in Church Street, Tiverton. In the summer of 1913, after having completed his six years with the Colours, he transferred to the Reserve and returned to Tiverton, that they might begin their life together. Six weeks later, on 19th September, having found employment as an insurance agent for the Pearl Assurance at 3 Fore Street, Tiverton, he gave notification of his intention to marry and the ceremony took place at the old Tiverton Registry Office, on 11th October 1913, in the presence of Louisa's father, Walter Land, a pensioner from the Heathcoat Lace Factory.

How we hope that those first few months of married life were idyllic, for the war clouds were gathering and in the following July, when the threat became imminent, he was recalled to army service. Leaving his 'Louie' and their new baby, Doris Winifred, with her family, he travelled to Newcastle to receive his orders and it was perhaps whilst there that he was promoted to Sergeant. A brief posting in Colchester preceded a period of training new recruits in the Midlands, by which time his young wife had been brought to the part of Croydon where he had grown up and they were thus able to be together again, whenever an army lorry travelling south provided the necessary transport.

Was it another of those cherished letters which brought the news of the birth of their first son, Jack Ernest, in April 1916 and was he at the Front by then, enduring the horrors of trench warfare? Or was Louisa listening still for the sound of the army lorry and was it the Battle of the Somme which finally tore them apart? That is something which we have yet to discover. For the attestment book states only that he fought in France and Flanders 1916–17. That entry does, however, tell us that by March 1918, when his second son, Reginald Walter, was born, he had been severely gassed. It was pointed out to us that the date of Reg's birth shows that Grandad was on leave during the summer of 1917, and must therefore have been gassed during the latter half of the year, almost certainly at the 3rd Battle of Ypres, otherwise known as Passchendaele .... It is a place which needs no introduction. The history books tell of the appalling conditions and of perhaps as many as 150,000 men slaughtered there. Grandad thought that he was one of the lucky ones, but not for long ....

Until the guns at last fell silent and even after that, he was at Catterick in Yorkshire, training new recruits, whilst supposedly recovering from the gas.

More than twenty years after she lost him, Grandma said softly, *'I can talk about it now. We were so happy when the war ended and he had come through it safely. But as time went on, it became obvious that the gas was still eating away at his lungs.'*

In 1919 though, that fleeting happiness was theirs still and whenever her 'Ernie' came home on leave from his northerly training camp, Louisa put her excellent culinary skills to use to provide a tasty spread, in spite of the food shortages. A pretty, dark-haired, dark-eyed girl, she would have looked her best, much of her time having been spent plying her needle to make clothes for herself and the children. Indeed, she made everything that they ate and wore. That Christmas may have been spent visiting her parents in Tiverton. Certainly there is evidence to show that the family were in Devon in January 1920 and Louisa's younger brother, Harry, safely home from the war and staying at their little terraced house in Limes Road, Croydon, is likely to have accompanied them.

When she first arrived in Croydon, Louisa had rented a

room from Mrs Rosa Lilley, further along the street at number 11, until suitable accommodation could be found and it was there that Jack was born in 1916. One of a terrace of twelve brick-built cottages with slate roofs and a single bay window, comprising three bedrooms, two reception rooms, a kitchen, a wash-house and a WC, this was built in 1881 and had both two-storey and single storey rear projections, but no back entrance. According to the 1910 Valuation Assessment Book, held by The National Archives, from which we obtained this description, the rent in 1910 for number 43 Limes Road, the home that Louisa made for Ernest whilst he was away at the war, was eleven shillings per week (55p). Built in 1884 and one of six slightly larger, red-brick cottages *with painted fronts, slate roofs and a single square bay window*, it comprised three bedrooms, the main one built over a passage between number 41 and number 43, two reception rooms, a kitchen, scullery, WC and cellars, and had a two-storey rear projection. This was the only home that the children had ever known and having heard them speak of their mother, I have no doubt that it was a happy one. She often took them to the parade ground to watch their father and Reggie, as he was then known, would crawl under the legs of the horses, his nappy trailing in the mud!

It was a time of decisions. Ernest's six years with the Colours and six years in the Reserve had come to an end and, keen to pursue a peacetime career with the army, he re-engaged on 3rd June 1920, for twenty-one years and was posted to Colchester. Now able to take Louisa out in the evenings, he took the trouble to set schoolwork for the children and sat up to mark it, however late he came home. He did not seem to mind how much he spent on pencils and writing books for them. Very good at figurework himself, he had worked up to become an acting Quartermaster Sergeant, of which he was very proud, and therefore wanted his children to do well, that they might succeed at whatever they chose, a trait which Jack inherited.

Ernest was a perfectionist and very particular about

everything – everything had to be just right – and there again his son took after him. It was he who inherited his father's fair hair and both took a pride in their appearance. Ernest wore a gold ring and diamond tiepin, which suggests that he liked to look smart and Jack grew up to be a very smart young man. If he knew why he was like he was, it will have meant a lot to him. For it is evident that though only a child when he last saw his father, he cared about him, perhaps more than anyone thought. Even when he was about to marry, Ernest was not forgotten. He asked his bride if she would mind having a bouquet of dark red carnations, his father's favourite flower, and if she would place the bouquet on his grave after the ceremony. During the invasion of France in 1944, Jack was blown up whilst checking for explosives in a mined building and as his hands tried to cling to the crumbling walls, Ernest's ring became embedded in the third finger of his left hand. Despite his injuries and the fact that he would lose the top of the finger, he begged the doctor to save the ring, as it was all that he had of his father. As time went on, his feelings did not diminish, for he cared enough to take me across to the War Memorial all those years later ....

I now have a photograph of the Dedication of the War Memorial at Eltham, in 1924 and just discernible in the background are three children of the right sort of age. The use of a magnifying glass has enabled me to see that the fair haired boy has the very hairstyle that Jack has in his early photographs and that he is sat alone on the church wall, looking as if his world has come to an end .... Was it him? .... I somehow think that it was ....

The day that he last saw his father must have started out just like any other. Except that Ernest may have been preoccupied with the forthcoming posting to India and may thus have been in haste, that the routine medical examination might be over the sooner and preparations made for the journey. He may only have glanced down in passing at the two little heads, one fair, one dark as like as not bent over a troop of tin soldiers and at the pretty little thing, so like her mother, perhaps stood at the window waving, as he went on his way. Yet that fleeting glance was to be his last. For he never came home again ....

Whatever his hopes, whatever his dreams, they were dependent upon the findings in that room and within minutes of closing the door behind him, he was left with nothing. I have tried to imagine what it must have been like. Yet how can I?

A photograph of the children has their dates of birth on the reverse side, together with that of his 'Louie', in what we think is Ernest's handwriting and judging by their ages, it seems likely that he had this with him in the hospital. It was all that he had. For he had left them that morning and never saw them again. Whilst he was a patient at the Royal Herbert Hospital on Shooters Hill, they were housed at the nearby Brookhill Married Quarters in Woolwich. Whether the army later met the cost of Louisa taking her family to stay in a small London hotel, whilst visiting her dying husband at the Colindale Hospital in North London, we do not know, but somehow or other that is where they were when Jack went to the bathroom, accompanied by Doris, and fell eighteen feet from the window, on to concrete! Rushed to Guy's Hospital, suffering from a fractured skull and a broken bone in his chest, he remained unconscious for six weeks and throughout that time was dangerously ill. Sadly, Ernest died on 20th March 1923, not knowing that his son was to recover after a year in hospital and thinking that *'he had brought Louisa to the workhouse'*. She was forced to move out of the Married Quarters and had nowhere to go, but thankfully Ernest's Commander-in-Chief handed her the keys to one of the Eltham hutments built for munition workers at Woolwich Arsenal, on the day that he was buried.

The change in Louisa is apparent from the photographs. There is one in which she looks almost stunned and I am guessing that it was taken just after she had lost him. For she is with her brother and sister and all three are in sombre attire. Another, taken in 1927, shows her older and thinner, no longer with any trace of the vibrancy she once had. The widow's pension took so long to come through that she had no money and was forced to sew tennis balls for Slazenger, at the rate of one shilling and sixpence (7½p) per dozen in order to feed the children. For several years her brother, Harry, brought in a wage to help support them, but mainly it was because of the efforts of their most devoted mother that they were well-fed, well-clothed and grew up to be happy and well-adjusted. Their 'ma', as children were wont to call their mother at that time, meant everything to them and most deservedly so.

And now, when I stand before the War Memorial at the eleventh hour on the eleventh day of the eleventh month, and think back to when I once stood there as a child, I can almost see those three solemn little children by the church wall. The chimes ring out across the busy street, but I see no cars or buses, only a long ago crowd and amongst them a young mother standing with bowed head beneath the old stone cross, whereon her husband's name is commemorated, her thoughts only of him throughout the Service of Dedication. Heartbroken, she had joined a Spiritualist Church in the hope of getting in touch with him again and attended séances. She seldom spoke of him, but perhaps she couldn't .... Her words, *'I can talk about it now ....',* more than twenty years after she had lost him, are indicative of that. She died in her home town of Tiverton in 1968 on the very day that he had died. Were her thoughts of him and had he come for her at last? We like to think so ....

*43 Limes Road, West Croydon, home of Ernest and Louisa
from late 1917 to late 1919.*

Doris, Reg and Jack (R), children of
Ernest and Louisa, about 1919.

The remaining half of the ring worn by Ernest William
Smith, the rest of which became embedded in his son
Jack's finger, when he was blown up in a mined building,
following the D-Day landings, 1944.

4

Croydon

Whilst recounting the search for Ernest William Smith, we have touched upon the lives of Edward and Emma Caroline, for in trying to find out who he was, we had had to uncover whatever we could about them. Some of the facts are thus strung out over the preceding chapters, but we now hope to draw these together, that their story might unfold.

We quickly found that Emma was the daughter of Robert and Sarah Craker of Croydon, the fifth of their eight children, but who was Edward? The marriage certificate had told us that he was the son of Thomas Smith, supposedly born in the early 1860s and we knew from Ernest's school admission registers that he must have died between July 1895 and September 1897. As there was only one possible General Register Office death entry for an Edward Smith in Croydon – the one in the September quarter 1896 – we sent for the certificate, but when it came, there was no definite proof that it was our Edward, as the address was 44 Cross Road and the informant was *'D May, sister'*, who had given an address in Epsom. Needless to say, we were most put out, but little did we know that this was the one vital clue which was to single Edward out from any other Edward Smiths in Croydon and that had Emma registered the death, we may never have got any further!

The most recent address at which we had found Edward and Emma and their family, was 92 Gloucester Road, in July 1893 (Percy's birth certificate) and, once we had established that their son, Ernest, and the one in the Sydenham Road School admissions register were one and the same, 1 Johnson Road in July 1895. But then we remembered that 44 Cross Road was the address at which we had found *'Mrs E. Smith, laundress'* in the 1897 street directory (compiled at the end of 1896), and as we knew for certain that the *'Mrs Smith'* in the 1898–1901 street directories was Emma, it seemed likely that this was her and that it was the right certificate. The proof that the Edward Smith who had died at 44 Cross Road was indeed our Edward, lay in the fact that he was buried in the same grave as Emma, but as our search for Edward's roots was taking place at the same time as we were trying to prove that their son, Ernest, was our Grandad, we had not as yet checked the cemetery records and therefore did not know that.

We had tried to find him in the 1881 Census by searching for Edward Smith, aged twenty, plus or minus five years, born in Reigate, living in Croydon. The age was based on that given at the time of his marriage, on Christmas Eve 1881, and the place of birth was taken from the 1891 Census. For although this was shown as *'Reight'*, there was no such place and we had therefore assumed that it was Reigate. However, only one Edward Smith was found – one which could not be right, as he was the son of a William and our Edward had given his father's name as Thomas on the marriage certificate. We therefore tried again, this time asking for those aged twenty, plus or minus five years, born anywhere, living in Croydon, and two were found – the one which we already had and another, lodging at 18 Tait Road. This was only months before Edward had given his address as Gloucester Road on the marriage certificate, and on looking at the street map of Croydon, we saw that Tait Road was a cul-de-sac off of Gloucester Road. Moreover, Emma's address, when she married him, was 3 Tait Road, which seemed rather a coincidence in a place the size of Croydon. It therefore seemed very likely that that was where they had met and that this was our Edward. But, if so, his place of birth was 'Leigh, Essex'! We studied a map of Surrey, however, and saw that there was a parish called Leigh to the west of Reigate! Was this yet another coincidence, or had the enumerator, who was perhaps not from those parts and did not therefore know that there was a Leigh in Surrey, added 'Essex' to the information given? We felt sure that he had and, in order to prove it, obtained a list of all Edward Smith births between March 1861 and December 1862 from the General Register Office index. There were very few in Essex and none anywhere near Leigh, whereas there was one born in Dorking, the next registration district to Reigate, in the December quarter 1861.

Pursuing another line of investigation – 'D. May, sister', the informant on the death certificate – Angela searched the 1901 Census index for Da...May, female; De...May; Di...May; Do...May and Du...May, as we did not know her Christian name. Amongst those found was Diana May, a widow aged fifty-three, living in Epsom, and as she was the only one in Epsom, we viewed the household and the address was the very same as that shown on Edward's death certificate. Her place of birth was Dorking. Excitement was mounting.

The General Register Office index was searched for the marriage of a Diana Smith to someone with the surname May and only one match was found – to William May in the March quarter 1867, in the Reigate district. Her birth could not be found, perhaps, it has since occurred to me, because we did not think to search for the earlier spelling – DINAH. We knew from Edward's marriage certificate however, that their father was Thomas and therefore looked for his marriage in the Dorking district from the start of registration to 1850 (to allow for the fact that the parents may have married after her birth). There were only two possibilities, in 1840 and 1847 and when we looked at the spouses and saw that there was a Dinah Simmonds in the relevant quarter of 1847, our hopes soared. Dinah/Diana was not a common name at that time and it therefore seemed likely that the daughter was named after her mother. We sent for the certificate, together with the marriage certificate of Diana May, which proved that she was the daughter of a Thomas, labourer.

The other certificate showed that Thomas Smith, a labourer, from the little Surrey village of Capel on the border with Sussex, son of Edward, had married Dinah Simmonds from Holmwood on 6th June 1847, at St John the Baptist Church, Capel. In the 1851 Census, they were living at Ryersh Farm, Capel, with their children, Dinah, aged three, born in Dorking, George and Emma. Another four children – Ellen, John, Thomas and Elizabeth – were born by the next census, but still no Edward. This tied in, however, with the possible birth entry in the December quarter 1861, as the census was taken in March. From the General Register Office index we obtained all Smith births in the Dorking district and by referring to the censuses, were able to work out which of them were relevant. Then at last, in 1871, Edward was found with his family – in Leigh. The census shows that he was a scholar, aged nine, born in Dorking, and that there were two younger children, William, aged seven, and Mary Ann, aged four, both born in Leigh. William was still at home in 1881, but by that time Edward was lodging at 18 Tait Road, Croydon with William Razzell and family from Charlwood, the parish adjoining Leigh.

We had two pieces of concrete evidence, which proved the identity of Edward, father of Ernest William – the marriage certificate which showed that he was the son of Thomas and the death certificate which showed that he was the brother of 'D. May', whose parents were Thomas and Dinah Smith. We were therefore now looking for the birth and/or baptism of their son, Edward, and happily, the certificate relating to the one registered in Dorking in the December quarter of 1861, turned out to be the missing piece of the puzzle. My Great Grandfather and Angela's Great Great Grandfather,

Edward Smith, was born in Holmwood on 24th September 1861, and was the eighth of ten children, five boys and five girls. Holmwood was an area of ancient woodland, south of Dorking, and until 1838, when the Church of St Mary Magdalene was consecrated, the baptisms, marriages and burials of the inhabitants were included in the Dorking Parish Register and marked accordingly. Thereafter, they are recorded in the Holmwood Parish Register and, whilst searching for Edward's baptism amongst those pages, we found a still-legible crasement of a pencilled-in entry which read *'Smith'* shortly after the date of his birth. The most likely explanation seems to be that, having arranged for the baptism to take place, either the child or the parents were ill and thus unable to journey to the church, which was some distance away. They may have meant to have him baptised at a later date but, as is evident from William's birth, the family moved to another parish within two years, if not immediately. For hiring fairs were held at Michaelmas (29th September) and Thomas could therefore have found work in Leigh straight after Edward's birth, which may have led to the baptism being forgotten. The fact that Edward was living in Leigh from the age of two years, or younger, explains why he thought that he was born there and put that in the 1881 Census and *'Reight'* (Reigate) in the 1891 Census, as Leigh was in the district of Reigate.

On Monday 24th June 1867, the weather was *'warm and very fine, causing work for the larger children in the hayfields and a corresponding influx of smaller children in the school'.* One of them was Edward. The logbook, held by the Surrey History Centre, records that there were twenty-three boys and twenty-three girls present on his first day and describes his early life within the walls of the little brick-built Victorian building on the edge of the village green at Leigh. The children were taught reading, writing and arithmetic, the latter being his elder brother Thomas's best subject, whilst his sister, Elizabeth, achieved nine out of ten in all three. In July, Edward was told the story of the man with the withered arm during his scripture lesson. The children were taken to Mynthurst for a school treat in August, and just before the harvest holidays, prizes which consisted of wearing apparel, books, pictures, maps and toys were given for attendance and merit. With the coming of Winter, rain and snow kept the *'smaller children confined to their homes'*, but Spring came at last and on May Day many children were *'absent with garlands'*. However, each of those who had turned up at school were given a penny. The logbook reflects the fact that education was considered of far less importance than the round of agricultural tasks, as attendance was low throughout June and July, due to an early harvest and once the acorns began to ripen, at the end of September, and for weeks thereafter, *'a large portion of the children'* were gathering *'the acorn harvest'* for fattening the pigs. 26th March 1869 was Good Friday and *'the children attended church and were each presented with a bun'*. We were then told of a wagon ride to the Industrial Exhibition at nearby Charlwood, on 19th May, and could not help but wonder whether this made such an impression upon Edward, that already the prospect of town life seemed inviting. As yet though, he was still only a boy and perhaps one of those *'severely reprimanded'* for *'trespassing for holly boughs'* as Christmas approached.

He grew up to be exceptionally tall. For a height of more than six feet two inches (cemetery records) is considered tall even now, yet during the 19th century, the average man stood five feet six inches to five feet eight inches. We found this interesting, as Grandad (Ernest William, son of Edward) was said to have been *'a big man'*, as were his sons, Jack and Reg.

The start of the Industrial Revolution a century earlier, had put new ideas into the heads of young men like Edward and many were now leaving the countryside to find work in the towns. Encouraged perhaps by the fact that someone he knew had gone to Croydon and was making his way there, he set off across the Surrey hills and when he came at last to the row upon row of terraced houses so different from the old, thatched cottages with which he was familiar, and was absorbed into the hustle and bustle of industry, he must have thought that it was indeed a place full of opportunities. In reality, life was hard and disease was rife, but as the part of Croydon to which he had come, was under development throughout the 1880s–1890s, there was work to be had and happiness was just around the corner .... Or, to be exact, further along Tait Road, where he was lodging with the friend from Charlwood. For as it was a close, the only way out was past the home of Emma Caroline Craker and it was therefore inevitable that they should meet. Love soon blossomed and they were married shortly after his twentieth birthday, at St James' Church, West Croydon. Edward's fine signature, shown in the parish register, suggests that he was accustomed to writing and one therefore wonders whether he sent a letter by way of the Penny Post to tell his family deep down in Surrey, of his new young bride. The discrepancy in ages, which later proved so puzzling, was apparent even then, inasmuch as Emma's age was given as eighteen years on the marriage certificate, whereas the census, compiled only months before, presumably by her father, shows that she was only sixteen!

The marriage having taken place on Christmas Eve, that must have been such a happy Christmas. They began their life together, there at 3 Tait Road, amongst Emma's family, and when the Autumn colours brightened the little garden backing on to the railway, she presented him with a daughter, who was given the fashionable name of Annie Amelia. A son, Frank Edward, followed in November 1884, by which time they may have been thinking of renting a home of their own and when one of the recently built terrace of fourteen brick and slate cottages in the next street came empty, they saw their chance. Thus their third child, Ernest William, was born at 185 Gloucester Road, in July 1887 and baptized on 18th September at St James' Church. Their new home had a front parlour with a bay window, a kitchen, scullery,

WC and three bedrooms, the third bedroom and scullery being contained in a two-storey back projection. The main bedroom was lit by two sash windows overlooking the street, and the garden backed on to open parkland.

Within a few short years though, the view had changed, as the rent was almost certainly beyond their means and, sadly, the child born in the smaller house further along the street and given the name of the Victorian songstress, Ethel Smith, was baptized privately in March 1891 and buried soon afterwards. The census reflects the change of fortune, in that Edward was then carrying coal, perhaps at the nearby railway, and Emma had returned to her former occupation of laundress, in an effort to supplement his earnings. If he was already suffering from tuberculosis, the scourge of such hard times, which was to claim his life at the early age of thirty-four, this may have affected his ability to work and meant that he had to find other employment.

Things seemed to improve though, if only for a while. For when registering the birth, some weeks earlier, of their last child, Percy George, in September 1893, he gave his occupation as builder's labourer once again.

Yet his days were numbered and in the Summer of 1895 the family moved in with Emma's parents, Robert and Sarah Craker, who were now occupying a three-storey house with a basement at 1 Johnson Road. Annie would have left St James' School at about that time to look for work, and whilst Frank may have remained there, eight-year-old Ernest transferred to the school at Sydenham Road, which was nearer to his grandparents' house. He may already have been showing an aptitude for arithmetic, as had Edward's brother, Thomas, and sister, Elizabeth, and his father may therefore have encouraged him in this, thus laying the foundations which later enabled him to work his way up in the army. It is evident from the subjects taught and from the progress reports at the end of each year, that Sydenham Road was an excellent school. For the object lessons listed throughout the logbook include circulation of waters of the ocean, Arctic exploration, railways – influence on trade, evaporation and condensation, our laws – how they are made, mode of supplying dwelling houses with gas and water, volcanoes – cause and effect, latitude and longitude, some ideas of the duty of a citizen, the water we drink – how obtained and purified, and forms of government in England (local, imperial) to name but a few and it is therefore not surprising that, if good at *'his sums'*, Ernest did well. In addition to the aforementioned subjects, the children also had to learn poems by Wordsworth, Longfellow and others of note for recitation, some of which comprised as many as 160 lines.

The report for 1895–6 reads:

'Discipline deserves praise and the elementary subjects are well taught, though reading might be improved. Recitation has been carefully prepared and the class subjects are highly satisfactory. Singing by note is creditable and shorthand is fair.'

And the following entries show how thorough the teaching was:

'4th November 1895 – Standards 5 and 6 examined in arithmetic, dictation, composition and drawing (freehand, model, geometry).'

'11th November 1895 – Standard 4 examined in reading, geography, grammar, recitation, mental arithmetic, music, map drawing, decimal notation and general intelligence.'

'19th March 1897 – Received report of Science and Art Department on drawing. This school marked 'Excellent' 8th year in succession.'

An interest in army training was promoted by regular *'Drill*

Inspections conducted by Sergeant Major Burke.' On 18th July 1895, Colonel Iredell was present and *'the competition drill company were taken first.' 'Six companies were inspected.'* The annual Drill Inspection on 16th July 1896, commenced *'at 4.15 pm during heavy rain'.* The comment reads *'for the past three years we have been unbeaten'.*

It wasn't all hard work however. For there were excursions to Bognor in July 1895 and to Worthing, Bognor and Eastbourne in June 1896 and as, at that time, most boys had never seen the sea, one can imagine their delight in rolling up their trouser-legs and splashing about in the shallows! Did Ernest tell his father what it was like and thereby bring a breath of sea air to those cheerless streets? For it seems unlikely that the outlying village schools, such as that which Edward had attended, would have arranged excursions even then, let alone in earlier decades, so he would not have known – and perhaps Ernest could see that now he never would.

As time went on, Emma rented a little house on the far side of the railway, where the air may have been cleaner and took in laundry to earn the money for food and medicine. A laundress since before her marriage, she would have known how to starch and goffer caps, collars and cuffs, polish starched shirt fronts and press long full skirts, and would have worked her fingers to the bone to provide this sort of a service, that she might earn enough to support Edward in his hour of need. His sister, Diana, was summoned to his bedside in the house in Cross Road, perhaps in the faint hope that she might somehow be able to nurse him back to health. But on Sunday 16th August 1896, in the midst of what would have been the harvest holidays when he was a boy in Leigh, not so long ago, his journey through life came to an end.

Emma struggled on alone, changing her address yet again, at which time Ernest transferred to Woodside School, where he remained until he reached the age of thirteen and started work as an errand boy. He was therefore one of those referred to in the governors' report for the year 1898–9 (Woodside School Logbook), which reads,

'The boys are in admirable order and the instruction is given with intelligence and success. Great care has been taken in drawing up the syllabus and in its systematic supervision.'

Several other entries in the logbook record that the annual Drill Inspection was carried out by Sergeant Major Burke in the presence of Colonel Iredell, as at Sydenham Road School. A letter from the former, headed *'Masters Must Note'*, gives an insight into the sort of physical training involved and the closing sentence which refers to *'marching or walking long distances or carrying weights'* suggests that this was designed to produce strong and healthy specimens and to be a preliminary to army training.

The School Admissions Register, now in the care of the Croydon Local Studies Library, shows that Ernest's younger brother, Percy, was also a scholar at Woodside and that he transferred to the upper school on 25th April 1902. There is, however, some doubt as to when he left there, although it may have been on 8th July 1904. No reason is given and we could find no trace of him thereafter. Was he the brother who later became a Sergeant Major and had a *'family up north'*? (as per my aunt in Devon). We hope one day to be able to answer that question.

Other snippets of information gleaned from the school logbooks, such as *'the great heat'* as the 19th century was drawing to a close and *'... the visit of Their Royal Highnesses The Prince and Princess of Wales ...'* whilst too trivial to have been recorded in the history books, nevertheless add a flavour of the times to one's family history. Photographs, however recent, also add colour. Thus, early one Sunday morning, before too much traffic was about, we photographed the houses in which Edward and Emma once lived and had the images printed in sepia, that that might tone down any modern features and afford the impression of an earlier time. Some have now gone, but we were able to find photographs of them, or of the relevant streets, amongst the excellent collection held by the Croydon Local Studies Library and obtained descriptions from the Valuation Assessment Books of 1910, held by The National Archives. Most were built to the same plan, but there were a few variations, such as a plumbed-in bath or a tiled forecourt. The Woodside Admissions Register shows that at the time that Ernest transferred to that school, Emma and her sons were living in nearby Exeter Road and the relevant street directory told us the number of the house. By the turn of the century however, they were occupying a newly-built house in Edward Road – the address in the 1901 Census – and were next found in another, also in Edward Road. Again the Woodside records had provided us with an address, as Percy moved on through the school, and their lengthy stay in this particular road suggests that Emma was drawn to the name. As time went on though, she flitted from place to place in the same area, her health now failing, until in the Spring of 1910, at the age of forty-six, the hard life finally took its toll of her.

Her son, Ernest, then serving with the Royal Field Artillery at Exeter, was about to find the fleeting happiness that The Great War was to put to an end. Whether Frank and Percy had survived the conflict we had continued to wonder and would have been wondering still, but for the kindness of the East Surrey Family History Society on the one hand and a chance discovery on the other. This last was so recent that we have not yet made contact with Percy's family, nor do we know exactly who or where they are, other than that he had a daughter, Rosemary, who married in Essex in the 1960s. It was a random death certificate that led us to him, as we had finally decided to obtain any which looked likely and trace the Percy named backwards through a marriage or the birth of a child or an address, in the hope of finding out who he was. If he was not ours, we would then send for another and so on and, in the absence of any relevant entries in Croydon, we had therefore chosen to begin with one in Lambeth, which was the nearest place, in the March quarter of 1971. We had not expected to know if it was our Percy, as we had no idea what had happened to him after he had left school, so it was such a lovely surprise to find his date of birth thereon. For although this useful practice seems to have started in the late 1960s, having had no occasion to send for a recent certificate, we were unaware of it. Another door has opened though, and we cannot help but wonder if, as well as finding out about Percy, we might somehow catch a glimpse of Grandad through it. So little is known of him even now, that a boyhood memory handed down through the years would be worth more than words can say.

Whatever memories his elder brother, Frank, had of his early life in Croydon, he kept to himself. He neither spoke of it, nor went back there and yet he must have cared. The proof of that lies in the fact that his son, born two years after the untimely death of his brother, Ernest, was named Edward Ernest. This son now lives in Canada, as does his brother, Frank William, and it is due to the efforts of their younger sister, Sheila, a member of the Buckinghamshire Family History Society, that we have now come to know this most welcome branch of our family. For our new-found cousin sought the advice of the representative of the East Surrey Family History Society, at one of the Buckinghamshire Family History Fairs, in tracing the descendants of her father's siblings. Five of their members' interests included the name of Smith in Croydon and one (ours) had specified the St James' district, where her grandparents were married. She was therefore instructed to write a letter, which the East Surrey Family History Society passed on to us. This illustrates how useful it is to join the family history societies, preferably in the county or counties from which your family come, as well as in your own area, that you may participate in the local projects, meetings and events. The quarterly journals contain interesting articles and useful information which may help with research, often include old photographs and describe the historical background of an unfamiliar county, and enable one to make contact with other members, some of whom may turn out to be related. The Family History Fairs are interesting and well worth a visit. There are representatives from many of the family history societies on hand to help with problems and search for a missing link in their databases of baptisms, marriages and burials and/or the census, etc. and stands offering computer software for sale, to enable you to draw up your family tree and store information electronically; other stands provide storage products for paper documents, plenty of useful literature and more besides.

This was thus the means by which Sheila was put in touch with us and as I was in the midst of the spring cleaning when her letter arrived, I asked my husband to read it aloud.

'To whom it may concern ... ' he began and thinking that it was just a general enquiry, I continued to apply the polish, but the moment I heard the words *'Frank Edward Smith'*, the letter was in my hand!

'It's Frank!' I cried, as if he had walked into the room. If only he had .... This was, however, the next best thing, in that his youngest daughter was searching for the family of his brother, Ernest William!

Until then, we knew only that he had disappeared between 1891 and 1901. We had tried to find him (using the method described in our search for Annie) but, as previously mentioned, the census seldom shows second Christian names and Frank was a popular name. Consequently, this resulted in page upon page of Frank Smiths. We viewed some of the households, but then it occurred to us, that if he was living with anyone other than relatives, we would never know for certain if it was him. It seemed probable that he had joined the army, as the barracks of the 1st Volunteer Battalion, Queen's Royal West Surrey Regiment were nearby, but inasmuch as he may then have met someone from further afield and never returned to Croydon, we had finally given up hope of ever finding him. Yet there he was .... It was a moving moment.

A hastily written letter brought a euphoric response and others, containing photographs of Ernest and his wife and children, and Frank and his were exchanged. Throughout most of my life, I had known nothing about my Grandad, yet there I was, looking down at a photograph of his brother! It was so hard to believe. One of the ones received, showed Frank's second son, Edward Ernest, at about the age that Grandad must have been when his army photographs were taken and there was a striking resemblance. (We later 'met' his eldest son, Frank William, via Skype and were struck by his resemblance to my Uncle Reg – Ernest's youngest son.) There in these letters and photographs was the long-lost link with his past and now at last that link had been forged again. It therefore seemed fitting that the meeting between us should take place in November, the Remembrance month. My one thought was, that if only Frank and Ernest could have been there .... but in a way they were, for they were there in our hearts....

In the Spring, Sheila flew to Canada to visit Frank's grave in the Chilliwack Cemetery, British Colombia, and tucked a photograph of Ernest down beside his memorial stone, that they might at last be together again.

When he left the house in Edward Road to join the army, Frank had just turned fifteen and Ernest was only twelve and a half. This must have been the last time that they saw each other. He served as a Private with the West Surrey Regiment in the Boer War and *'was known as the youngest man on the column, and .... was a committed signaller and busy both nights and days'*. Whilst serving in South Africa, he was ambushed by forty or fifty Boers, captured and held prisoner on a farm until the end of the war. He was released 160 miles from the British lines and was in the middle of a *'trackless desert'* losing consciousness when rescued by Bechuanaland border guards who had fortunately seen vultures circling overhead.

Soon after his return to England, in 1902, he joined the Royal Field Artillery and was posted to India where he became a Staff Sergeant and learnt to speak Hindustani and Pushtu. The British Army paid 120 rupees and 800 rupees to anyone who learnt these languages. A reservist at the outbreak of the 1914–18 war, he was sent to France with the Army Service Corps and was part of the retreat from Mons. He was wounded four times in two wars, and was captured by Germans but managed to escape alive, as he was a fast runner! After his discharge in March 1920, he became a bus (tram?) driver based at Hammersmith Bus Garage. Two of his three sons emigrated to Canada during the 1950s, and when widowed he too emigrated at the age of ninety and died there in 1979.

We are fortunate in that we have now seen a photograph of Frank and are thus able to picture him, but there are none which can tell us whom Annie resembled, or whether she was pretty. Although it is almost certain that she had beautiful hair – later referred to as *'the Smith hair'*.

I first heard this expression, when Grandma remarked on my waist-length tresses, which were my mother's pride and joy, and told a little story. Often repeated over the years, this found its way into my family history notebook, but was long forgotten by the time that we were searching for Annie in the 1901 Census. As I have already said, we were up against the fact that second Christian names are seldom shown, and that Annie was a fashionable name. Moreover, if her employer had completed the census, she could have been shown as Ann. However, determined to try, we put in *'born in Croydon, living in Croydon'* and as she was not at home with her mother and brothers and was therefore likely to have gone into service, *'born in Croydon, living anywhere'*. Things were complicated by the fact that, because of a change in the county boundary, Croydon had transferred from Surrey to London, which meant that we also had to try *'born in Surrey, living in Croydon'*, *'born in Surrey, living in Surrey'*, *'born in London, living in Croydon'* and *'born in London, living in London'*. This resulted in page upon page of Annie Smiths, none of whom seemed at all hopeful. Nevertheless, the households of any which were even remotely possible were viewed, but she was not there! Yet we knew that she must have lived at least until the end of the 1914–18 war, as my aunt remembered her, so was there an error?

Her mother having had no head for figures, the most likely explanation seemed to be that either she had been told her age incorrectly, or that she too had had no head for figures and had therefore given the wrong age. Or perhaps eighteen had been mis-transcribed as '28'. These further possibilities were explored, but still no luck. Finally, in desperation, Angela put in *'Smith, female, age 18, born Croydon, living anywhere'* and fifteen matches were found. Fourteen of these were named – none Annie – the other one read *'.... Smith'* and was a general domestic servant living in Croydon. We viewed the household, which included Henry Marshall, a chemist in Addiscombe Road, his wife and children and two servants, one of whom appeared to be *'Alhnie'* Smith, aged eighteen, born in Croydon. As this was not a name, it had not been transcribed, which is why it came up as *'.... Smith'*. This illustrates how important it is to allow for every eventuality and not to be too restrictive in your choice of criteria when using online search facilities. Still unfamiliar with Croydon, we referred to the street map and when we saw that the shop, with living accommodation above, was only about two minutes' walk from 44 Cross Road, where Edward had died, and was even nearer to Edward Road, where Emma and her sons were living at the time of the census, we were indeed hopeful. The more so when, at the mention of a chemist's shop I suddenly remembered the story behind *'the Smith hair'*! Out came the long ago notebook and the relevant entry was found. In my mother's words, *'Someone in Grandma's family, at the turn of the century'* had had such beautiful hair, reaching right down to her ankles, that she was asked to advertise Harlene Hair Drill. Apparently she sat in the window of a chemist's shop, with her back to passers-by, combing her hair, the product beside her. For there were, of course, no television or radio in those days. Manufacturers were reliant upon newspapers, periodicals and billboards to make their products known, so what better way for a retailer to increase his sales, than by persuading a servant girl with exceptionally pretty hair, to help out simply by sitting in the window of his chemist shop, combing her hair. She may have received a higher remuneration and would certainly have been excused from her duties whilst thus occupied.

My mother had assumed that Grandma (formerly Louisa Land) was referring to someone in the Land family, when she spoke of the girl who had advertised Harlene Hair Drill, but then why call it *'the Smith hair'*? For were I to refer to something belonging to anyone from my side of the family, I would not use my husband's name to describe it. I therefore feel sure that she was speaking of Annie Smith. The timing is exactly right as, according to the Internet, Harlene Hair Drill was in use around the turn of the century, at which time Annie would have been eighteen years of age. The strange entry is easily explained, in that as doctors are notorious for their illegible handwriting, perhaps the same may be said of chemists. A busy man, Henry Marshall may have filled out the census form in haste and if the person transcribing it could not read his writing .... It is certainly a possibility, and if one takes into account the fact that my father had such beautiful hair that it would have been the envy of any woman and that, in his mother's words, *'He was the one who was like his father'*, it becomes much more than a possibility....

But what happened to Annie? It seemed that by 1911 she

was no longer employed by the chemist, and the fact that she could not be found in the 1911 Census, yet was known to have been alive after the 1914–18 war, suggested that she married between 1901–1911. However, as there were no marriages in the Croydon district amongst the pages of Annie Amelia/Annie A. Smith General Register Office entries, (the second Christian name is not shown after 1909), we hoped to narrow these down by referring to the census. If, for example, an Annie Amelia/A. Smith had married 'Joe Bloggs' in Chelmsford in 1906, we looked for an Annie Smith in Chelmsford in the 1901 Census and if one was found, it seemed unlikely that that was the marriage of our Annie. If not, we searched the 1911 Census for Joe and Annie Bloggs in order to find out her age and place of birth and by this means managed to reduce the number of possibilities. Yet there were still too many to enable us to decide upon a certificate, and, as by this time the pathway to the past was enticing us onwards, the search was set aside. There was still hope though, as our new-found cousin, Sheila, the daughter of Frank Edward, provided us with a vital clue. For she had noticed that one of the witnesses on her father's marriage certificate was <u>Annie Amelia</u> Barker and it seemed too much of a coincidence that Frank should have known someone with exactly the same Christian names as his sister well enough to have asked her to witness his wedding. For although the name Annie was fashionable, when coupled with Amelia, it was much less common. The initial euphoria was dampened however, by the fact that no marriage of an Annie Amelia Smith to a Mr Barker could be found in the General Register Office indexes. The handwriting on the General Register Office copy of the certificate having been difficult to read, Sheila sent for a further copy, whereupon the name appeared to be Barber. We all thought that that would solve the problem, but no Barber marriage could be found either! This pointed to it being a second or subsequent marriage and the next step was thus to obtain all marriage entries for Annie Amelia/Annie A. Smith prior to the date of Frank's marriage, as well as all those for the surnames Barker and Barber marrying an Annie Amelia/Annie A. with any surname, that we might compare the two sets of surnames in the hope of finding a match. For example, if our Annie Amelia (Annie A. if after mid 1909) had married 'Joe Bloggs' and he had died, she would then have been Annie Amelia/A. Bloggs when she married Mr Barber. We had therefore to find the name of 'Bloggs' in both lists in order to arrive at a possibility, whereupon we would need to send for the two certificates in order to establish whether our assumptions were correct. At least we now knew that, as she had put both of her Christian names when witnessing her brother's wedding, she was likely to have done the same when she herself was wed.

There were 102 Annie Amelia/Annie A. Smith marriages, 25 marriages between a Mr Barker and an Annie Amelia/Annie A. of any surname and 4 marriages between a Mr Barber and an Annie Amelia/Annie A. of any surname, yet there was only one match! In the March quarter of 1907, Annie Amelia Smith married Chris Warren in the Watford district, and there was a subsequent marriage between Annie A. Warren and William J. Barber in the Brentford district. The parish register entry for the Smith/Warren marriage in Bushey, told us that the father of this Annie Amelia was Edward! At the time of the 1911 Census, Chris and Annie Warren were visiting someone in Chepstow and we discovered from this that he was a rock builder, aged twenty-seven, born in Hoddesdon, Hertfordshire, that they had been married for four years, which fitted with the marriage entry already found, and that she was aged twenty-eight, which meant that she was born in 1882–3 in <u>Croydon</u>! Our Annie was born in October 1882 – in Croydon .... We checked the General Register Office indexes and there was only one Annie Amelia Smith born in Croydon – ours .... The marriage certificates of Annie

Amelia Smith and Chris Warren and Annie A. Warren and William J. Barber were therefore requested, and having seen from the General Register Office indexes that an Edward B. Warren, whose mother's maiden name was Smith, had been born in Croydon in the December quarter of 1911, we also requested his birth certificate. The result was 100% success!

The first certificate showed that Annie Amelia Smith, daughter of Edward deceased, supposedly aged twenty-two and living in Bushey, Hertfordshire, had married Chris Warren (unusual though it was at that time, he was actually baptized 'Chris', which was fortunate in that there was no mistaking him), a rock builder, aged twenty-two from Hertfordshire. Once married, she must have confessed to a minor deception, as the 1911 Census records her correct age, twenty-eight, by which time her husband was twenty-seven. From the second certificate we learnt that a son, Edward Bell Warren, had been born on 3rd December 1911, at 22 Freemasons Road, Croydon to Chris Warren, artificial rock builder, and his wife, Annie Amelia, formerly Smith. We looked up the address in the Croydon street atlas and saw that Freemasons Road was part of a crossroads – directly opposite was Cross Road where her father, Edward, had died, whilst running east-west was Lower Addiscombe Road, and the chemist's shop wherein she had advertised Harlene Hair Drill was thus but a stone's throw away. Sadly, little Edward Bell died within weeks and there were no other Warren children with the mother's maiden name of Smith born in Croydon, which seems to suggest that they moved away.

Annie's second marriage took place in Brentford, Middlesex on 22nd August 1934 and we now know that this was not far from where Frank was then living. They must therefore have kept in touch and it was because she witnessed his marriage to Winifred Charlotte Buckman and his youngest daughter, Sheila, noticed the names 'Annie Amelia' on the certificate, that we were finally able to trace her. One thing remains a mystery though. For when marrying William James Barber, Annie Amelia Warren, daughter of Edward Smith (deceased) was described as a widow, BUT we recently came across the death of Chris Warren in the General Register Office indexes in 1950! – and the certificate shows that he was the right one.

Can she have thought that she was a war widow? For the nature of the warfare during the 1914–18 conflict was such that many men were blown to pieces by the shelling and mines, and therefore disappeared without trace. Consequently, if he deserted or suffered a head injury which resulted in temporary loss of memory, and disappeared for that reason, the authorities would not have questioned it, as they would have assumed that he was one of the fatalities, and Annie would have been notified. If he had tried to find her years later, but she had moved to another area or remarried by that time, he would not have known where to look and it would therefore have been impossible. Or did she just pretend to be a widow, when she saw her chance of happiness, in order to assume an air of respectability, as there was such a stigma attached to divorce in the 1930s? Even after the Second World War, such things were whispered behind closed doors. The divorce records, held by the Principal Registry of the Family Division, may tell us the answer, but whatever the reason behind it, the marriage to William Barber lasted nearly thirty years and therefore seems to have been a happy one.

When searching for Annie's death in the General Register Office indexes, now that we knew her surname, we came up with three possibilities: aged seventy in Edmonton in the March quarter of 1948, aged seventy-nine in Ashford in the June quarter of 1962, and aged eighty in Colchester in the March quarter of 1969.

Although the age was wrong, the one in Edmonton seemed the most likely, as it was in the London area. Moreover, the General Register Office indexes contained twelve births of Warren children with Smith as the mother's maiden name in the Edmonton district between 1913 and 1923 (two couples from 1918) and the first of these was an Edward, so it looked as if Chris and Annie had left Croydon after the death of little Edward Bell Warren and had gone to live in Edmonton. She could then have remarried in Brentford when widowed and later returned to Edmonton, where she ended her days. But surely she would have brought one or more of her children with her when visiting her brother's wife and children, yet my Aunt had never mentioned that. We therefore decided to check for a marriage of a Warren male to a Smith female in Edmonton just in case, and two came up, just prior to the birth of the first child on our list. Consequently, the other two Annie death entries, both of which were the right age, were now looking the more likely and, by chance, we plumped for the correct certificate. Annie died at 19 Lower Denmark Road, Ashford on 26th May 1962, and the moment I read that, my one thought was that my father was still alive then and that had he known where she was, he would have taken me to meet her. Perhaps then, though the years had passed, I would have seen for myself the reason for the phrase *'the Smith hair'*.

*Marriage entry from the parish register of St James' Church, West Croydon, showing Edward Smith's well-written signature at a time when education was still in its early stages.
2809/1/14, Copyright of Surrey History Centre.
Reproduced by permission of Surrey History Centre.*

St James' Church, West Croydon, where Edward and Emma were married on Christmas Eve 1881 and their children were baptized.

185 Gloucester Road, West Croydon, birthplace of Ernest William Smith.

Frank Edward Smith (1884–1979), brother of Ernest.

5

Fresh Fields

Long before we thought of a way of tracing Annie, or were given the means by our new-found cousin, we had set off for the Surrey History Centre, in search of the records which would enable us to follow the pathway to the past down through the Surrey hills. For Grandad's father, Edward Smith (1861–1896), was born in the Holmwood, an area of ancient woodland south of Dorking, and the census showed that <u>his</u> father came from even deeper down in the Surrey countryside, amid the fields and farmsteads near the Sussex border. Not that we were expecting to get anywhere with a name like Thomas Smith! However, we knew from the marriage certificate, acquired when trying to establish the identify of his son, Edward, that he had wed Dinah Simmonds, daughter of William Simmonds of Blackbrook on the edge of the Holmwood, on 6th June 1847, at St John the Baptist Church, Capel. We therefore began by searching for their children's baptisms in the parish registers pertaining to Capel, Dorking, Holmwood and Leigh. According to the censuses, these were the children's birth places, Holmwood having come under Dorking prior to 1838, which was probably why they still thought of it as such, when giving the details to the enumerator. It was whilst searching for the family in the parish registers and in the later censuses, that we began to appreciate how unusual and therefore useful the name of Dinah was, as there was another Thomas Smith in the same parish at the same time, but because our Thomas was coupled with Dinah, he was singled out in whichever records they were found. Without her, we would have got no further, so how thankful we were that he had chosen her, rather than someone with as common a name as his own!

The census traces their movements from Ryersh Farm in the parish of Capel, near the Sussex border, northwards to Holmwood, as Thomas found work as an agricultural labourer. Though the farms depended upon these men, as they could turn their hand to anything from the most menial tasks to the most arduous, such as harvesting and haymaking, the wages were low and times were hard. They ploughed the fields, sometimes walking as much as sixteen miles a day, sowed the seed, tended the crops and prepared the feed for the animals and a hundred and one other jobs were crammed into the long hours expected of them. Yet it is said that in some ways it was a happy life. At harvest time, as the school logbook records, Dinah and the older children would also have worked in the fields, that they might supplement Thomas' earnings and it is evident from some of the entries, that in farming communities work on the land and seasonal chores took precedence over education. Notwithstanding this, the children seem to have been intelligent and must have worked hard at school, as some of them continually achieved top marks in Arithmetic and English.

Great Great Grandmother Dinah and the new young Queen, were almost of an age and, like her royal counterpart, she too raised a large brood of children. Sons George, John and Thomas and daughters Diana, Emma, Ellen and Elizabeth were born by the time of the 1861 Census and Edward, from whom our line descended, followed in the September of that year. It looks as if Thomas found work on a farm near the picturesque village of Leigh, at the Michaelmas Hiring Fair, held on the 29th of that month. For before their newborn son was baptized, he loaded the cart and moved his family northwards again. Another son, William (to whom Edward was probably close, as he named his second son, Ernest <u>William</u>) was born in Leigh in 1864 and their youngest daughter, Mary Ann, in 1867. Still with a long life ahead of her, Dinah, in her straw bonnet, worked on the land ruled over by the Queen in her beribboned one and was the more fortunate of the two, in that though Victoria's beloved Prince Consort succumbed to pneumonia at an early age, Thomas strode on into the 20th century. Along the way, he must have seen many changes, amongst them the invention of photography and it may thus have interested him to know that, at the start of yet another century, his Great Great Granddaughter and his Great Great Great Granddaughter were following in his footsteps, recording on film anything which recalled those times. The little schoolhouse at Leigh, for example, and the water-pump on the village green nearby, at which Edward and his brothers and sisters would have refreshed themselves before returning home on hot summer days; the various churches where the baptisms, marriages and burials took place; the stile set in the church wall and an ancient cottage which, in its youth, must surely have seen our family pass by. On we went, in search of Nalderswood Dean Cottage in the district of Horley, assisted by some old Ordnance Survey maps provided by the Horley History Group. For it was there that we had found Thomas and Dinah and their youngest son, William, in the 1881 Census and, living with them, Frank and Emma Sale, the children of their widowed daughter, Emma. At that time, Thomas was working at Stumblehole Farm in Nalderswood, which was marked on the map and our journey ended in the nearby hamlet of Ironsbottom, where he and his Dinah spent their twilight years.

By 1891, the Sale children had gone, Frank having been about to enlist in the Royal West Surrey Regiment and work his way up to become a Colour Sergeant, serving in South Africa, India and Australia; whilst Emma married a jockey from Epsom and moved to Newmarket. The later censuses show that they were blessed with eight children, but that she was widowed by 1911 and we learnt from his death certificate that her husband, Richard Drake, had come to a terrible end beneath the wheels of a traction engine at the age of forty-one. Returning to her grandparents however, in 1891, they were sharing their home in Ironsbottom with her other brother, George, and had taken in an agricultural labourer as a lodger, as was the custom amongst Victorian farming families.

Those were the years of change. The horseless carriage had recently been invented and during Thomas's lifetime, the speed limit was raised, thus allowing these dangerous contraptions to tear about the countryside at 20 mph! He would not have known that man's dependence upon the horse was coming to an end though, or that the tractor would soon change the method of farming so dramatically. For after nearly sixty years of marriage, the moment of parting came at last on 21st August 1905. He was laid to rest in the quiet country churchyard at Sidlow Bridge, Horley, just around the corner from their cottage, and Dinah went to live with her daughter, Elizabeth Ball, in the village of Brockham. The introduction of old age pensions allowed her to retain a degree of independence and, as time went on, she too would have seen changes. Already the Edwardian woman had discarded the crinoline and bustle in favour of softer lines and her more militant sisters were soon to join the Suffragette movement and resort to drastic measures in an effort to have their say. A generation of young men marched away to war and the newspaper casualty lists reflected the tragic consequences. With grandsons at the Front, Dinah must have been one of the millions who prayed for peace and whilst listening, incredulously at first, to voices coming from a box known as the wireless and watching even more incredulously as the amazing new flying-machines were taking to the skies, may have whiled away the hours looking back. Her long life had spanned five reigns and on a summer's day, in the midst of the peace celebrations, it finally came to an end.

The parish register containing the date of her burial at Sidlow Bridge, and that of Thomas, was still at the church and therefore required a postal enquiry, which also brought forth a plan of the churchyard showing where they lie, the familiar fields all about them. At nearly ninety-seven years of age, Dinah had lived long enough to have known her great grandchildren in Croydon, but one wonders whether she did .... or whether they knew of her ....

Thomas's early life, before he met Dinah, held the key to the past, but it was her unusual name that enabled us to find it. There on the marriage certificate and in every one of the censuses, that name left not a shadow of a doubt that we had found the right Thomas Smith and thus led us back along the path afforded by the parish registers. The aforementioned sources had provided us with Thomas's place of birth, approximate date of birth and his father's name and as he had been born prior to registration, we made our way to the Surrey History Centre in search of his baptism. The relevant entry was found on 19th December 1824, in the transcript of the register for Capel, a parish down near the Sussex border, and a note in amongst further entries relating to Thomas' siblings, Peter (1822), George (1827) and Mary (1830), showed that this was then largely farmland. For it says that if the father of the child being baptized was an agricultural labourer, no occupation was given and as the relevant column was almost always left blank, this is an indication of just how many of them were living in the parish in those far-off days before the invention of the tractor. One such was, at that time, Thomas' father, another Edward Smith, who became known as 'Old Edward', as he was further back than the Edward who was the father of Grandad Smith.

Already the search for the children of 'Old Edward' and Ann had covered a lengthy period both before the baptism of the first known child, Peter (1822) and after that of the last known child, Mary (1830), but had yielded nothing.

Having therefore assumed that there were no other children, we expected to find their marriage just prior to Peter's baptism, but this further search, although extensive, also yielded nothing. Had the truth become known, 'Old Edward' was full of surprises! To begin with, not only had he not married in the parish, but by referring to the Surrey marriage index, we discovered that he had not even married in the county and our hands were thus momentarily tied. The roots of the tree were so well hidden that we were going to have to dig deeper, but the branches were now starting to flourish. For our best hope of tracing a name like Smith was, we felt sure, to set out the whole of the field before us, as with the 800 Ernests, and we had therefore begun extracting all Smith baptism, marriage and burial entries from the Capel parish register and from those of all of the nearby parishes and compiling them into little family trees, showing each couple and their children. As time went on, these fitted together to make bigger trees, to which information from the censuses was added and we were surprised to see how many of the Smiths in that part of Surrey were actually ours. During the course of this, we had chanced upon an interesting marriage entry in Capel in 1837, just prior to registration, that of a James Smith, son of Edward. As far as we knew, 'Old Edward' did not have a son by that name, but, that said, he was the only Edward Smith in Capel. In fact, he was the only Edward Smith in any of the parishes anywhere near there, including Dorking, which was very much larger, as the only one found there, turned out to be him! Thankfully, at that time, the name of Smith was no more common in the little village of Capel than any other surname – indeed less so than some – and there were very few Edwards of any surname.

Consequently, still puzzling over this James, we suddenly remembered a James Smith, born in Capel, who was living with Thomas and Dinah at the time of the 1861 Census. Was he the son of the James, son of Edward, who had married in 1837 and therefore Thomas' nephew, and his father

82

Thomas' elder brother? Fortunately, the aforementioned James, son of Edward, had married a Lucy (those Smith men were so helpful!) whose name, like the name Dinah, was most unusual and therefore, just as Dinah had always led us to Thomas, so Lucy always led us to James. The baptisms of their children were thus easily found and the first of them turned out to be the James who was living in the house with Thomas. Hoping that the census would help to determine whether James Senior was the son of 'Old Edward', we looked for him in 1851, as the earlier one would only have told us whether he was born in the county. However, the entry was misleading, as the place of birth was shown as Alfold, yet no baptism could be found there. The later censuses were therefore checked and the place was in fact Ashtead. The earlier entry was obviously a mistake on the part of the enumerator, as James' baptism was found in Ashtead on 16th March 1817. Hopeful that there might be more children and that that might help to pinpoint the date of the elusive marriage of 'Old Edward' and Ann, we checked the rest of the parish register, using the fiche produced by the West Surrey Family History Society and came across another daughter, Hannah, baptized 12th September 1819. But why there, north of Dorking? Had 'Old Edward' had to go that far in search of work? Or was there some other reason? .... An article cut from the pages of a family history magazine, told us that 1816 was known as *'the year without summer'*, as it was so cold. The bad weather had an adverse effect upon the harvest and thus upon the livelihood of those working on the land and may therefore have led to the journey northwards. There could have been more to it than that however, but for the moment we were concerned only with the fact that James and Hannah had proved that their parents, the Edward and Ann Smith who were having children in Ashtead 1817–19, were our 'Old Edward' and Ann, who were having children in Capel 1822–1830. In the case of James, a James Smith, son of Edward, ('Old Edward' was the only Edward Smith in Capel or anywhere near there) married Lucy in Capel in 1837 and her unusual name ensured that we found the right James Smith in the censuses, which told us that he was born in Ashtead. The baptismal entry in Ashtead showed that he was the son of Edward and Ann and there was a note beside it which read, *'No abode or occupation given'*. This suggests that the couple were new to the parish, as there is no such note beside Hannah's baptism and it only occurs against a few other entries. At the time of the 1861 Census, James, the eldest son of James and Lucy, was living with Thomas and Dinah, whilst his parents were living in the cottage which 'Old Edward' had vacated, in Henfold Lane, Holmwood (which until it became a parish in 1838, had been part of the parish of Capel). Until then, they had been occupying another house further along the lane, but, when widowed, 'Old Edward' had given his cottage at Stockrydons Farm to his eldest son, James, and had taken himself off to the Dorking workhouse. Having queried this at the Surrey History Centre, we were told that this was commonplace amongst elderly widowers, as they no longer had someone to take care of them.

In the case of Hannah, her marriage entry at Holmwood in May 1841, shows that she was the daughter of Edward Smith, labourer, of Holmwood and the 1841 Census, compiled the following month, confirms that 'Old Edward' was the only Edward Smith then living in Holmwood. Later censuses give the address of Charles and Hannah Flint (formerly Hannah, daughter of Edward Smith of Holmwood) as Betchworth, which was at that time a hamlet just off of Henfold Lane, and Hannah's place of birth is shown in every census as Epsom, and Ashtead is just outside Epsom and comes under that district.

At about this time, we made a brief sortie into local history and found that it added interest to the family history. Equipped with the census as our guide, a camera with which to photograph any buildings or other features, which still looked as they would have done during 'Old

Edward's' lifetime, and a notebook in which to record the name, approximate age and situation of every house in that long lane, we set off to find where he was living. The 1841 Census had given us the location of his house and the earliest Ordnance Survey map had shown us in detail, what that outlying part of the parish of Capel was like at the time. It would then have been just a track without a name of course, but has since become known as Henfold Lane, probably because Henfold Farm is situated at the southern end. This having retained its name, it seemed like a good place to start our investigation, as the houses which had changed were able to be identified by their age and position in relation to those which had not. Using the census to direct us, we made our way from one end to the other, taking down the details as previously mentioned. These were later compared with old Ordnance Survey maps and with the tythe map compiled in 1839 and we were thus able to establish the whereabouts of Stockrydons Farm and a pair of cottages belonging thereto, one of which 'Old Edward' had once occupied. The cottages had gone, but a row of late Victorian cottages had been built on the site and on part of the adjacent plot and these had been given the name Stockrydons. The Ordnance Survey maps and censuses enabled us to work out an approximate date of construction, by pinpointing the changes, and through these we learnt that James and Lucy were still living in 'Old Edward's' abode in 1871, but by 1881 had become the occupants of one of the newly-built four-roomed cottages, the one on the site of their former home.

Still uppermost in our minds, whilst all of these little pieces were fitting together to create a picture of the past, was of course, 'Old Edward's' marriage and perhaps even his baptism. Whether such a thing was remotely possible, we did not dare ask ourselves. We just kept looking and hoping. To begin with, the probable date of the marriage was around 1820, but now that the baptisms of James (1817) and Hannah (1819) had come to light, it was likely to be around 1816, or earlier, and that therefore opened up a new line of enquiry. For whilst extracting all of the Smith entries from the parish registers, we had come across a Jane, daughter of Edward and Ann, baptized 25th October 1812, and a Harriett, daughter of Edward and Ann, of Holmwood, baptized 4th December 1814, both in Dorking. At that stage, we had not known where 'Old Edward' was living and such a long gap between these dates and the baptisms of his children in the adjoining parish of Capel (1822–1830), had made it seem unlikely that he was the father, but now that James and Hannah had been fitted into that gap, that was no longer the case. Moreover, this was an Edward and Ann and we had not found any other Edward Smiths in that part of Surrey, let alone one married to an Ann. In order to prove that the Edward and Ann Smith who were having their children baptized in Dorking 1812–14, were 'Old Edward' and Ann, we had to try to trace the daughters.

There were, however, only two entries relating to Jane, that which recorded her marriage to James Webb in 1830 and the baptism of their daughter, Mary Ann, in 1831, against which were the words, *'of Holmwood'*. This was good though, as the Jane Smith daughter of Edward baptism, was in the Dorking parish register, as Holmwood then came under Dorking, whereas she was now described as *'of Holmwood'* and 'Old Edward' was the only Edward Smith in Holmwood. But no further help could be gleaned from Jane, as her family were not to be found in the 1841 Census. Emigration seemed a likely possibility, but we could see no point in pursuing this, inasmuch as a name on a passenger list would be of no use to our present line of enquiry.

Harriett was therefore our only hope, although sadly the proof lay in the fact that she died at the early age of twenty-five in the Dorking Workhouse and was taken to Holmwood to be buried. The death certificate gives no clue to her parentage, as she was a servant and the person registering her death would not therefore have had that information.

There were, however, only two Harriett Smiths of the right sort of age in that part of Surrey at that time, and as the other, the daughter of a John, was living in Dorking with her family, there was no reason why she should have been taken to Holmwood. The burial in October 1840, therefore had to be that of the Harriett daughter of Edward and Ann of Holmwood, baptized 4th December 1814 in Dorking – and in the 1841 Census, we then found 'Old Edward' living in Henfold Lane – Holmwood .... The plan of the churchyard shows that Harriett is buried in a shady corner by the track – now the Dorking to Horsham road – along which he must often have passed and just across that road, beyond a strip of woodland, lies Henfold Lane. Not all of the names in the burial register are included in the plan, but it is thought that both 'Old Edward' and Ann are buried with their daughter, as it was pointed out to us that the grave shown thereon is considerably bigger than those which were to accommodate only one person.

One step nearer to finding the elusive marriage, we were now looking around 1812 and having seen from the map that Capel was almost right on the Sussex border, a telephone call was put through to the West Sussex Record Office. There were some long and anxious minutes whilst the archivist checked the Sussex marriage index on our behalf, but then, Eureka! Edward Smith had married Ann Field in Horsham on 21st March 1812. We knew from the census, that the Ann who had married 'Old Edward' was born in Capel around the 1790s and turning now to the Capel parish register, found an Ann, daughter of James Field, baptized 6th November 1791. A further search confirmed that she had not married in the parish, nor was she buried there, although her family had remained there. At the earliest opportunity, we visited the West Sussex Record Office, that we might look at the Horsham register and a search thereof told us that there were no baptisms of an Ann Field prior to the date of the marriage. Nor were there any other Field entries throughout this period, which shows that the Ann who married Edward Smith was not from there. But did they stay there? In order to find out, we carried out a search covering a period of 100 years from the date of the marriage and there was no mention of either an Edward or an Ann Smith. This fitted with the fact that 'Old Edward' and Ann's first child was born in Dorking later that year and that both were buried in Holmwood. During the course of this, we had made a note of any Field entries and the only ones found were of particular interest. For Ann, daughter of James Field of Capel, whom we now thought had married Edward Smith, had a brother by the name of William and these entries showed the marriage of a William Field, carter, on 12th March 1812 (nine days before the marriage of Edward and Ann) and the baptisms of his daughters, Sarah (1814) and Eliza (1816). This William Field was then found in the Capel parish register. His daughter, Sarah, was buried there in August 1820, aged six, and another daughter, Sarah Ann, was born there in 1821. This therefore links the Capel family of Fields with the Sussex town of Horsham, which is literally just down the road from Capel, well within walking distance and not much further than Dorking, and it suggests that brother and sister, William and Ann, had gone there to find work and had married there within days of each other and later returned to Capel. According to the copy of the marriage licence, sent to us by the staff of the West Sussex Record Office, 'Old Edward' was then working as a servant to William Wood, husbandman, so it seems likely that Ann was either a servant in the same household, or in one nearby, and that was how they met. We thought it interesting that she was descended from John Caryll/Carryll, wheelwright of Rusper, and might therefore be related to the Knight by the same name, from the adjacent parish of Warnham, who has a monument to his family in the chapel which he had built in the church there. These are the Carylls referred to in *'Catholicism and Community in Early Modern England'* – Michael C. Questier – a line worth tracing perhaps ....

although at that time, there was something of far more importance to us – 'Old Edward's' greatest surprise of all.

Until now, we have referred to the census only in passing, that we might leave this until last, but it was actually during our very first visit to the Surrey History Centre that it came to light. It was near the end of the day and the clock was marching on. We had never expected to get anywhere at all with the name of Smith, yet had somehow reached back to the 1820s and did not want to have to leave there without at least trying to find out something about this new-found Great Great Great Grandfather. The last few minutes left to us before the doors of the Surrey History Centre closed, were therefore spent viewing the 1841 Census, in the hope of finding Thomas still living at home, that this might identify his father. Instead we actually found his father. Thomas had already gone off to find work as an agricultural labourer, but George (13) and Mary (11) were still at home and their ages were exactly right. 'Old Edward's' age had been rounded down to fifty-five and Ann's age was forty-five, as in this census only, the age of an adult is rounded down to the nearest five years, whereas the age of a child is supposedly correct. John, aged nine, came as a surprise to us, but his baptism was later found in Newdigate in 1832 and a little detective work provided an explanation. Apparently, the parish boundary between Capel and Newdigate crosses Henfold Lane, in which 'Old Edward' was then living, and as the nearby church at Holmwood had not yet been consecrated, rather than walk to the village of Capel, he must have just decided to walk in the opposite direction when having his youngest child baptized! However, our interest at that moment was centred upon the column headed 'Born in the County?' as beside 'Old Edward's' name was the letter N!

It was then that we first saw from the map how near Capel was to the Sussex border and although we did not yet know that he had married there, we thought, of course, that we were going to have to go there in search of his forebears.

But there were so few minutes left and we had to know the place – if he had lived long enough to say! Fortunately, though small, with enough incentive, Angela can be fast and the 1851 Census was before us in not much more than a flash. Still (thankfully!) an agricultural labourer in Capel and still the only Edward Smith in the parish – and, for that matter, in any of the parishes anywhere near there – 'Old Edward' was easy to find and as we stared down at the column headed 'Where Born?', I could almost hear him saying in a deep, throaty voice, 'BUCKENHAM. SARTON LEE'!!!

South Holmwood, near Dorking, Surrey.

Vicarage Lane, Capel.

The school on the village green at Leigh,
which Edward Smith attended from 1867.

6

Sarton Lee

Buckinghamshire!!! We were not only amazed, we were incredulous! We knew where it was, but that was about all – and as for Sarton Lee .... we had never even heard of the place! I can remember thinking, as we sat there at the census reader wondering what to do next, 'Why couldn't it have been Sussex? Or if it had had to be Buckinghamshire, why not Aylesbury?' At least we might have had some hope of finding that and Angela voiced the very same opinion. But how wrong could we have been!? For 'Old Edward', Bless him, could not have helped us more. As we may never have found a Smith in a town such as Aylesbury, let alone in well-populated Sussex – not even an Edward Smith – but he came from a hamlet. Although as yet we did not know that. Still trying to think what to do, Angela reached for Arthur Mee's *'The King's England'*, but Sarton Lee was so small that even he had not come across it! Yet still we had not realised what a good thing that was ....

A telephone call in search of advice, was put through to the Centre for Buckinghamshire Studies in Aylesbury and we were fortunate in that Rachel Simon, to whom I spoke, was very knowledgeable and most helpful. I have to admit that I was daunted by what she had to say though. There was no such place as Sarton Lee!!! Not in Buckinghamshire anyway and 'Old Edward' had been most definite about that. The census entry had read, *'Buckenham'*. Could I find out more from the 1861 Census, she asked, and I remember saying that he was <u>old</u>. He may not have lived that long. But I had not allowed for his determination! No wonder he walked all that way to Surrey! Old or not, nothing was going to stop him from letting people know where he had come from!

The General Register Office indexes had yielded a possible death at about the right age, in the Dorking district in the March quarter of 1865, but was it him? Rather than wait for the certificate to arrive, we hurried off to The National Archives, in search of the 1861 Census, so much depending upon the outcome, that until the all-important entry was before us, we could think of nothing else. There he was though and almost at once I was reaching for the telephone to tell Rachel Simon that this time he had put down, 'STAUNTON LEE'. However, just as we had feared, that did not exist either! She put the name of Edward Smith into the Buckinghamshire database, and presumably his approximate date of birth, and it came up with a baptism in 1782 in Saunderton Lee. This Edward was the son of a John, whom she found in the Posse Comitatus in 1798, along with another John Smith and a Richard Smith, all of whom were labourers living in Saunderton Lee. The excitement was such that I hardly dared breathe. Was it 'Old Edward' and, if so, how would we ever prove it?

At least there was hope and we therefore put our heads together and devised a plan of action. A visit to the Centre for Buckinghamshire Studies was of course our first priority, as we had to find the baptism of the Edward Smith from Saunderton Lee in the parish register and we were hoping that there might also be entries relating to his parents and any siblings. Most importantly though, we were looking for his marriage and burial. Although how we hoped that we would not find them! For as 'Old Edward's' marriage licence had stated that he was a bachelor, if this Edward had married in Buckinghamshire, he could not be 'Old Edward' and similarly if he had been buried there, as 'Old Edward' was buried in Holmwood in 1865.

Joining the Buckinghamshire Family History Society was also a priority and, having done so, we realised that, contrary to what we had at first thought, we were so fortunate in that 'Old Edward' had come from Buckinghamshire. For the Family History Society have done everything possible to help the researcher and are constantly adding to their resources. At that time, their database of pre-1837 marriages was complete and the baptisms and burials of most of the parishes were covered and for a small fee, one could obtain a printout from the relevant database as follows: single surname search, all parishes, 100 year period; single surname search, six parishes, all years. (A further option – all parishes/all years – has since been added.)

A postal service whereby one may borrow transcripts of the parish registers of parishes not yet included in the database, helps to fill in the gaps and also covers Oxfordshire parishes which border on Buckinghamshire. All of the aforementioned services are of such a great help to those living some distance from the Record Office and they had recently implemented a further means of assistance, in that members at a distance qualify for two hours free research by volunteers per annum. Indeed the Family History Society are both helpful and knowledgeable and altogether excellent, to say the least.

One of our first moves upon becoming members, was to borrow books and data from the postal library service and on enquiring about a book entitled, *'The Place-names of Buckinghamshire'*, we were told that this was not available on loan, but could be checked on our behalf by the librarian, Adrienne Thirkell. Consequently, 'Old Edward's' problem was explained and back came a reply, bringing good news indeed. For she had said that LEE would be right, as he had put that twice, whereas the other word had obviously been recorded incorrectly, and there were only three places in the whole of Buckinghamshire the name of which ended in the word Lee – Saunderton Lee, Shipton Lee and Nash Lee. He must therefore have come from one of them! The reference to the place having been recorded incorrectly reminded me of something which we had been told by a 1914–18 war veteran some years earlier. He had been recalling his experiences in the trenches and had mentioned that the regional accents were so strong at that time, that the officers had had difficulty in understanding what the men in their command were saying. Thus how much harder must it have been in the previous century, when people moved around even less and the accents were therefore thicker still? Both of the census enumerators were likely to have come from Surrey, or thereabouts, and being unfamiliar with 'Old Edward's' broad Buckinghamshire brogue, would have written down what they <u>thought</u> was said, rather than what was actually said. Moreover, they would also have been unfamiliar with Buckinghamshire places and could not therefore have hazarded a guess as to which of them he was referring to.

By this time, we had acquired another extremely useful book entitled, *'Buckinghamshire Dialect'* – H. Harman, which explains that in the Buckinghamshire of the past, those who were from there did not pronounce the middle syllable. This meant that the word Saun/der/ton would have been shortened to Saun/ton. The book goes on to say that AU was pronounced AR (example given – daughter pronounced darter) which makes Saun/ton sound like SARN/TON. I then tried rolling the R, as those with a country accent would have done at a time when regional accents were very much thicker, and having tagged LEE onto the end, found that the N was swallowed up and what I heard was SARTON LEE!!! Perhaps as 'Old Edward' grew older still and had therefore spent many more years amongst those with more southerly Surrey accents, his brogue was not quite as thick, hence the place name given in the 1861 Census. Or maybe it was just that the 1861 enumerator was either better or worse at spelling. Whichever it was, things were looking good for the Edward Smith baptized 1782 in Saunderton Lee.

However, we have both always prided ourselves upon thoroughness and therefore had an enormous task ahead of us. All Smith entries from every parish in the databases were obtained as follows: *Burials* – 1782–1882 (allowing for him to have been 100 years old). *Baptisms* – 1722–1821 (the hundred years prior to Peter's baptism in Capel in 1822, as 'Old Edward' was there by then). *Marriages* – 1723–1822 (as before, but allowing for him to have married in Buckinghamshire before going to Surrey and having Peter baptized).

Peter's baptism was used as a guideline, as when we first discovered that 'Old Edward' was from Buckinghamshire, we had not yet proved that the earlier children, baptized in Dorking and Ashtead, were his, nor had we found his marriage in Sussex. The reason why there were Smith entries prior to 'Old Edward's' birth, is because the Family History Society provided the service covering 100 years of each parish and we thought that those reaching back to 1722 would be of more use to us in tracing other members of the family, than the later years, after he was known to have been in Surrey. We also needed to know to which Edward Smiths, born prior to 'Old Edward' as well as afterwards, the marriage and burial entries could relate.

The parishes which were not yet included in the databases, were checked either at the Record Office, or by making use of the parish register postal service and we used a map of the Buckinghamshire parishes to record our finds. No marriage or burial had been found for the Edward Smith in Saunderton (this is the name of the parish; Saunderton Lee is a hamlet within the parish of Saunderton), nor were there any other Edward Smiths in the parish. But in case he had gone elsewhere in search of work, or there was one, or more, born in Shipton Lee or Nash Lee, and they had gone elsewhere, we had to check all of the other parishes. Fortunately, the parish priest usually made some mention of where an outsider was from. Thus the search began and, as you may imagine, we were holding our breath throughout!

For future reference, if an Edward Smith was found, that parish was coloured in blue on our parish map. If not, but there were Smiths there, it was coloured in red, whereas if there was nothing relevant, it was coloured in yellow. This also enabled us to see how much of the county we had yet to cover. We were careful to note down details of any Edward Smiths, as we had to establish when and where each one of them was born, if he had married and where, and where he was buried. Thankfully, as in Surrey, the name of Edward was not common, although there were a few more of them here. The 1782 Saunderton Lee Edward had disappeared, but was he in Surrey, that was the question. Things were still looking good, inasmuch as there were no Edward Smiths born in either Shipton Lee or Nash Lee at around the right time – and 'Old Edward' had been adamant about 'Lee' and Buckinghamshire! There were still several Edwards in other places to investigate though. Most were subsequently found to have married and/or had been buried in the next, or a nearby parish, with some reference to where they were from and even if further afield, the burial entry read, for example, *'of Wendover'*.

The Strays lists compiled by the Family History Societies, which record those from one county who have been found in another, had already been checked for the 1782 Edward, as had the Settlement Certificates, many of which have survived for Buckinghamshire. For at the time in which we were interested, anyone who went from one parish to another needed one of these, as it was an assurance that if the person fell on hard times and became a drain on the new parish, the former parish would accept responsibility. One of these confirmed that an Edward Smith living in Buckingham, had gone from Padbury to Buckingham with his wife, Elizabeth, in 1818. (We also found their marriage in Padbury in April 1818 and both were *'of the parish'*.)

Another Edward Smith had died in Great Marlow in 1847, at the age of forty-two and although the age was nowhere near right, as he was *'of Saunderton'* (the parish, not the hamlet of Saunderton Lee), we felt that we had to send for the death certificate, just in case the parish register entry had been mistranscribed. Thankfully though, this Edward was indeed aged forty-two and as our potential Edward would have been nearly sixty-five at the time and could not possibly have been thought to have been so much younger, he was ruled out.

That left one. One upon whom so much depended, that I shudder to think of it. You can imagine how we felt. He had died in Buckingham in 1873, at the age of ninety-one, and was not born there and our potential Edward, the one baptized in 1782 in Saunderton Lee, would have been ninety-one in the December of that year! We were so near to the end of our search, so close to claiming him as our three-times (and four-times) Great Grandfather, that the waiting and wondering whilst we tried to find a clue, were absolute agony. For unless we could prove that the one in Buckingham was not the aforementioned 1782 Edward, we could go no further. But what could we do? We were both beside ourselves with anguish. But Angela, thankfully a little less so, came up with an idea. The 1871 Census. If only we could find him, that would show his place of birth. A visit to the Centre for Buckinghamshire Studies was hastily arranged and calmly she inserted the reel. Long minutes seemed longer still and when the name finally appeared, it was that of some other, much younger Edward Smith and then of yet another. There he was at last though – and how I wish that that dear old man could have known how much happiness he would one day bring, just by telling the enumerator that he was born in <u>Watford</u> ....

For figuratively speaking, that one word led us along the little lane winding its way through the wheatfields to the hamlet of Saunderton Lee. All of the records had been checked most thoroughly and there was no doubt whatsoever that Edward, son of John and Ann Smith, who had once lived in the end one of six farm cottages there, had tramped the rutted packways to a more southerly county in search of a better life. In Horsham, he had met his Ann, whilst working for a Husbandman there, but it was in Surrey that they had put down roots. Did he ever long to go back? In 1816 perhaps. Certainly he had gone further to the north of the county in search of work, but then his wife gave birth to their third child, a son at last, and if she too was homesick, he may have relented and turned round. The arrival of more children at regular intervals, would have made the prospect of undertaking such a journey even harder to contemplate, until one day the carrier may have brought word that his mother had died and perhaps he thought that it was then too late. For there he remained, working in husbandry and on the land until a great age. It seems though that he never forgot that far-off land of golden wheatfields. For in Henfold Lane, Holmwood, to the south of what is shown on an early map as 'Darking', there is a 1940s house called Bradenham, beside the Victorian cottages on the site of that in which 'Old Edward' is known to have lived. It is not a name which anyone unfamiliar with Buckinghamshire would think of, but the houses are built where fields once were and in the past fields had names .... one the name of the hamlet in which 'Old Edward's' eldest brother was living at about the time that he left home perhaps. He may have ploughed those fields and there may thus have been others named after other Buckinghamshire hamlets where his family were living. We shall never know, but that one word leads us to wonder. For along the edge of that one-time field is a hedge[1], laid in the old way, the Buckinghamshire way .... It was the only one in that area and the only one in that part of Surrey, but in the country lanes but a stone's throw from Saunderton Lee, that method of hedge-laying still survives.

1 An article referring to the different methods of traditional hedge-laying throughout the country, illustrated the South of England method, which did not resemble this hedge; whereas hedges at The Chiltern Open-Air Museum in Buckinghamshire, showing the method used there, were exactly like it.

We were there at last, stood at the edge of the field which 'Old Edward' must have crossed in his youth, after closing the cottage door behind him. There was no one about. Nothing stirred but the ripening wheat bathed in the rosy glow of sunset. It was a place so evocative of times gone by, that it could have been another century. His mother might almost have been there at the window still, watching until he was out of sight and we wondered, with a touch of sadness, how often, in her advancing years, she had climbed the stair and looked longingly across the field to Wycombe, in the hope that he might one day return. Perhaps she had exacted a promise from him at the moment of parting, but bound by the ties of his new life so far away, he never came ....

There in Buckinghamshire, our family tree grew to vast proportions and to it were added some most unusual and thus interesting Christian names, such as Jeptha, Archelaus, Jabez and Free. As with Dinah and Lucy in Surrey, whenever the name of Jeptha was found, the family proved to be ours and this was indeed a boon.

'Old Edward' was the youngest of ten children – seven sons and three daughters – and most of these moved away from Saunderton Lee and formed sturdy branches of the tree in the nearby villages and hamlets. His eldest sister, Salley, married Joseph Benning of Ellesborough and the aforementioned Archelaus was the eldest of their three children and was named for his paternal grandfather. The next sister, Ann, was perhaps close to Salley, which may have been why she went to live in Ellesborough and found work there, but sadly she died at the early age of twenty-eight.

'Old Edward's' eldest brother, William, was called upon to serve with the Militia, a trained band maintained by each county, and at that particular time England was in the midst of the Napoleonic Wars and there was a threat of invasion. Lots were drawn and if a man either could not serve, or did not wish to, he could pay someone to take his place and this

William seems to have done. However, he was obviously not averse to doing his bit, as he then took the place of another, Thomas Wright, which leads one to wonder whether – if a slightly higher fee was charged on the second occasion and the balance was shared with John White, the friend who had replaced him – this was an 18th century means of increasing one's income! He had married Sarah Stallwood from Bradenham in 1789, but was soon widowed and was living at Naphill when he transferred from the Militia to the Army on 24th July 1799. We have yet to find his service record, that we might perhaps discover what happened to him thereafter.

The Eureka Partnership have published a great many interesting little books which contain transcriptions of lesser-used sources, and some of these which we found useful in tracing our family and filling in interesting details, are as follows: *Royal Buckinghamshire Militia, Men Discharged 1799 and 1807*; *The People of Princes Risborough* (2 volumes); *The People of West Wycombe*; *Posse Comitatus Lists 1798* (one volume for each hundred); *The People of Bledlow* (2 volumes); *Persons Named in Wills Proved 1736–1857 – Peculiar Court of Thame and Great Milton* (other courts and dates are covered in the series).

To give an example of the contents, the sources included in *The People of Princes Risborough*, Volume 2 are: Subsidy Roll 1673, Poor Rate Assessment 1777, Militia Ballot List 1796, Recipients of Chibnall's Charity 1801–1820, Poor Rate Assessment 1812, 1831 Census, Dutton, Allen and Co's Directory 1863.

From this we learnt that another of 'Old Edward's' brothers, Richard, was also called upon to serve with the Militia in 1796, but his place was taken by the third son, Joseph, of whom nothing further is known. Richard's wife, Sarah (Blick), from Princes Risborough, was about to present him with a second child at this time, which was probably why Joseph went in his stead. Soon afterwards, Richard and Sarah moved into the end cottage at Saunderton

Lee with his parents and as he is named in the Enclosure Records, this enabled us to establish where the family were living. He and his father and younger brother, John, were agricultural labourers and would have had to work from 5 a.m. to 7 p.m. for a paltry wage, perhaps as little as 12d (5p) per day. They were employed on the farm at Saunderton Lee when listed in the Posse Comitatus compiled in 1798. This was once a countrywide record arranged by county of all men aged fifteen-sixty years, who were able to take up arms if the need arose, but has only survived in entirety for Buckinghamshire. Divided into Hundreds and then into the parishes within those Hundreds, it is contained in a series of small books published by the Eureka Partnership and there is a name index which enables one to find all the entries relating to a particular surname. These entries show a man's full name and occupation and the parish in which he was living. Occasionally there are references to an infirmity, or to a man being over the age but insistent upon being included. It is a unique record of the adult male population of the county and was thus later to prove invaluable to us, when searching for the baptism of 'Old Edward's' father.

However, at this stage we thought that we had come to a standstill and would get no further now that we had come up against a John Smith. Consequently, we were concentrating on broadening the family tree by tracing the lines of descent from 'Old Edward's' siblings. As in Surrey, we were compiling little family trees from the parish register extracts, using the Buckinghamshire parishes map, coloured in during the Edward Smith search, as our guide to where there were Smiths. The pages and pages of baptism, marriage and burial entries from all of the parishes covered by the Buckinghamshire Family History Society database and those extracted from the parish registers available on postal loan and from those at the Centre for Buckinghamshire Studies, which were not yet included in the database, were now put to further use and the censuses provided us with still more information. The whole of Buckinghamshire had already been checked for Edward Smiths, during which time we had made a note of anyone from Saunderton, or any of the nearby parishes, who had married, or was buried, further afield, for future reference. Thus we were now only concerned with the relevant parishes – those in which our family had been found and those in the vicinity of Saunderton. The resulting family trees showed all of the Smiths in Bledlow, Bledlow Ridge, Bradenham, Ellesborough, Great Kimble, High Wycombe, Horsenden, Hughenden, Lacey Green, Monks Risborough, Princes Risborough, Radnage and West Wycombe. They began with each couple and their children, but as time went on, some became parts of our tree, whilst others fitted together to make several different family trees which, for ease of reference, we named according to an unusual occupation therein, such as, 'The Ratcatcher' and 'The Corndealer'.

This having enabled us to establish which Smiths were ours, our tree had grown to a tremendous size, yet still three of 'Old Edward's' brothers were missing. We know that James (baptized 1780) married Mary Green of Princes Risborough in 1802, but he then disappeared. Nothing is known of Joseph, except that he took Richard's place in the Militia, and Thomas could have been one of several, none of whom reached the 1851 Census which would have shown their place of birth. The fruitless search for these three, coupled with the fact that only two of 'Old Edward's' siblings lived until the earliest census, made us realise how extraordinarily lucky we were, that he had not only got that far, but had gone on, thus providing us with the information from the 1851 and 1861 Censuses, without which we would never have known who he was. Why he left Buckinghamshire, has so far still eluded us. Although whilst trying to discover the whereabouts of the parish records pertaining to Saunderton, we were handed a scrap of paper which may have pointed us in the right direction. There were but few words written thereon, yet we were struck by the content, inasmuch as it provided a link between the cottages at Saunderton Lee and the place to which he had travelled. Brief details of a sale of the entire terrace were given and it seemed such a coincidence that the owner of property in such a small and obscure place as Saunderton Lee, should be from Crawley in Sussex, which is in close proximity to <u>Horsham</u>. We could not help but wonder whether the fact that this family owned property in both places, had anything to do with 'Old Edward' uprooting and moving to Horsham. Was it that he might work on their land there instead? This is something which we hope one day to look into.

Interestingly, the paper also told us that the purchaser was the son of 'Old Edward's' sister, Mary (1775–1841), who had married Benjamin Avery, a farmer from Radnage, in 1799. The 1841 Census, compiled only weeks before she died, shows that she was living in High Wycombe at that time, with Christopher, the youngest of their eight children, and it therefore seems likely that she sometimes referred to the cottage in which she was born and those in which her family were also living and that that may have influenced him to buy them when the opportunity arose.

The row of four-roomed cottages at *'Sarton Lee'*, which 'Old Edward' had left behind, featured prominently in our family history throughout the long reign of George III, those of George IV and William IV and the early years of the reign of Queen Victoria. For it was there, in the end one overlooking the fields, that John and Ann Smith raised their ten children, of whom 'Old Edward' was the youngest, and when widowed, Ann remained there with her son, Richard, and his family until she died in 1825, at the age of eighty-three. The third cottage had long since been occupied by her younger son, John, and his wife, Elizabeth Blick of Princes Risborough, who is thought to have been the cousin of Richard's wife, Sarah. The baptism of the first of their nine children in Princes Risborough in 1795, and the Posse Comitatus in 1798, in which John is listed as an agricultural labourer in Saunderton Lee, determine roughly when they came there, and as they were still there in 1841, the census enabled us to discover in which of the cottages they were living. After his marriage to Elizabeth Wellard, their son, William, moved into the adjoining one, but must have later found work on another farm, as that would account for the fact that he moved to Small Dean, in the nearby parish of Bradenham, taking his ageing parents with him. For it was there that they ended their days.

Their many sons and two daughters settled in the villages and hamlets thereabouts, Thomas having married Leah Wellard, Edward and Samuel, sisters Martha and Sarah Brooks from Bledlow, John Mary Ginger from Saunderton, Sophia Joseph Penn from Great Missenden and James Nash from Prestwood Common, and their eldest son, James, Mary Lacey, Sarah Sales and thirdly Jane Jifkins of Chinnor. Our research has touched upon all of these surnames, albeit briefly, that we might add a little more colour and interest to the family tree.

By far the most interesting Christian name which our research has uncovered, is Jeptha, an unusual Biblical name given to the son of James Smith (1795–1869), the eldest son of John and Elizabeth. Not only was this an unusual name, but it was an extremely useful one to trace. Jeptha Smith, born in 1815, was easily found in every census from 1841–1891, living either in Loosley Row, Old House, or at nearby Wardrobes Farm in Lacey Green, and often led us to others thereabouts, who were also members of the family, but may otherwise have been overlooked, if their names were not Smith. We were always so pleased to see Jeptha there on the page, that that may be why his name conjures images of a large and likeable character and inasmuch as the name was later given to the sons of his brother, his uncle and a cousin, that may well have been what he was like! Sadly, one of them died as an infant and another at twenty-one, but old Jeptha and the son of his cousin journeyed on through the 19th century and were of great help to us, as were the unusual names of his son, Jabez, and Free Currell, who married his daughter, Elizabeth Jane in 1894.

We were, of course, still hoping to reach back further into the past, but as previously mentioned, 'Old Edward's' father was a John Smith (!!!) and was not from the parish .... Thus with time on our hands, whilst trying to think if there was any way in which we could try to overcome that, we were taking an interest in the places where our family had once lived. New to Buckinghamshire, we found it captivating. It was like a treasure trove of lovely little hamlets hidden amongst the fields and hedgerows. Even the signposts leading to places we had only ever seen on a map or in the database, were steeped in excitement and, having found our way there, it was almost as though we had caught a glimpse of how things once were. The lane to Wardrobes, which Jeptha must once have trodden, and the little church where he was wed, were captured on film, as were the houses strung out along a nearby hillside, which the census describes as Loosley Row. Also unchanged were the many other churches wherein our family's baptisms, marriages and burials had taken place and some old farm buildings nestling at the foot of the hill leading from Lacey Green, which after a closer look at the map, turned out to be Small Dean, where John and Elizabeth had ended their days. A building on the road to West Wycombe was clearly once the Workhouse and wherever we went we came upon farms, historic features and picturesque villages recalling the past. Even an ancient footpath enticing us onwards and calling us back. There was a surprise around every corner, not the least of which was how near to each other these places were. We had thought that they would be miles apart, but most were literally only just down the road from each other, a fact which was about to have a bearing upon our research.

For a decision had at last been made. We had come up against the name which had become something of a standing joke amongst family historians – and indeed it was no joke! The path to the past had disappeared before our very eyes and we would now never know what lay at the end of it. By this time though, we had finished wallowing in self-pity and were reminding ourselves that we had found Grandad Smith, against all odds, even if it had taken almost a lifetime! We deliberately did not remind ourselves that there were only 800 Ernests, whereas there were probably an awful lot more John Smiths in the whole of Buckinghamshire! For, working on the assumption that 'Old Edward's' father was not from too far afield, or the Vicar would have made a note of it when recording his marriage to Ann Giles in 1764, we were again setting out the field before us, as with the 800 Ernests. The fact that there was no note in the register, suggested that John Smith was known in Saunderton and that he probably worked on the land somewhat regularly. At that time, there were no Smith baptisms, marriages or burials in the parish, other than the marriage of a Thomas to a girl who was from there, thus our John was from somewhere else. However, there were John Smiths in almost every village anywhere near there and the only clue that we had, was that he was aged sixty years or under in 1798, the date of the Posse Comitatus. This had therefore provided us with a maximum age and in order to arrive at a minimum age, we took into account the date of the marriage. We were, however, aware of the fact that although a marriage can now take place at the age of sixteen, with consent, the lawful age was much lower in the 18th century, (before 1929 girls could marry at twelve and boys at fourteen) and this had to be taken into consideration. Gordon Honeycombe, the presenter of the 'Family History' series in 1980, had referred to someone in his family who had married at the age of fourteen in the 1840s, his bride being nineteen, and although it seemed most unlikely that our forefather had been so very young, we had had to allow for that. Our field of research therefore included all John Smiths baptized in any of the parishes within reasonable distance of Saunderton Lee, between 1738 (aged sixty at the time of the Posse Comitatus) – 1750 (aged fourteen at the time of marriage) and in case he was unsure of his exact age, any baptized just before. (As there were no birth certificates at that time, people had to rely on events when trying to recall a date. For example, 'the year of the great storm', 'the year without summer' or 'the year of the bad harvest'.) Possibilities were found in High Wycombe, West Wycombe, Princes Risborough, Monks Risborough, Bledlow, Hughenden and Radnage, and in the Oxfordshire parishes of Chinnor and Towersey, as Saunderton Lee was so close to the border between Buckinghamshire and Oxfordshire, that some of these were nearer than some of the Buckinghamshire parishes. We had only just realised that, having visited the area once again, to see exactly how near, or how far, the places in question were from there. All were certainly within walking distance and one has to remember that people were much more accustomed to walking in the 18th century than they are in the 20th – 21st century. Moreover they did not use the roads, as we do, but footpaths across the fields. Consequently, Oxfordshire, which heretofore we had thought of as another county and therefore out of the question, was found to be not much more than a stone's throw from Saunderton Lee. So we could not even rule out the ones from there!

We had got as far as compiling large-sized index cards for each of the John Smith baptisms, showing the date and place, the parents' names and any other information given, such as the father's occupation. There were further cards covering events such as marriages, showing the date, place and the name of the spouse. The baptism of a child or children, were put onto a separate card, or if a John Smith witnessed a marriage or a document, that too was given a card, showing the date, place and any other names mentioned. Every available piece of information relating to a John Smith was recorded. The sources included the censuses, Bastardy Bonds, the Posse Comitatus, Poll

Books, Settlement Certificates, Poor Rate Assessments, the Militia Ballot List and Wills. Each burial entry was put onto a card, along with the date, place and any relevant details, such as *'pauper', 'son of....', 'junior'* etc., and *'wife of John Smith'*. We even included those who could not be ours. The Corndealer from Princes Risborough for example. He had a definite burial stating who he was and as our John also had a burial, they had to be two different men, but he had had to be included as some of the events could have applied to him, rather than to one of the other possibilities. Similarly, the baptisms of those who could not be ours were recorded, as the burials could have related to them and possibly some of the other events. Consequently, we had a pile of cards ranging from 1683–1798 (the hopefuls having been marked with an asterisk) and in order to ensure that all of these John Smiths were accounted for, we had had to cover a much longer period when extracting the burial entries from the parish registers. Fortunately though, from 1813 onwards the age is shown, which meant that we had only to note down those which were relevant (ie none relating to children). The purpose of this was to try to eliminate some of the possible baptisms, as any John who had a definite burial, or was married at the time of the marriage to Ann Giles, could not be ours. When all of the information had been put onto the cards therefore, the John Smith baptisms were arranged along the length of the table and we tried to match them with the events and burials. Some, such as the one baptized in Princes Risborough in 1744 ('the favourite'!) and the one baptized in 1748/9 in West Wycombe, had definite information which excluded them and this was fixed to them with a paperclip. Others were probable, but we could not be certain and some could have applied to more than one John. Consequently, all of this was inconclusive and the search would therefore have ended there, had Angela not suddenly come up with a brilliant idea!

Following Hardwicke's Marriage Act of 1753, a new

form of parish register came into use, which required both parties to sign, or make their mark, in the presence of two witnesses and thankfully our John Smith had signed when wed. Angela's idea was therefore to obtain a photocopy, or digital photograph, of his signature and of the signatures of any other John Smiths who had signed, either in the marriage register or on some other document, that we might compare the signatures and would perhaps be able to work out who had done what. Fortunately, most had signed and even those who had put a mark were useful, inasmuch as our John could write – very well, as had Edward more than a century later – and any document upon which someone had made a mark, could not therefore be attributed to him. Each of the signatures, and even the marks, were given a letter – A. B. C. etc. – which was also written on the relevant marriage index card, so that we knew that the signature of the John Smith who had married Mary Walker, for example, was D. The baptism cards were then arranged along the length of the table, in chronological order, as before, and beginning with the earliest one and the earliest marriage entry, we applied the one to the other and asked ourselves if he could have married on that date. Not whether he was likely to, but whether he could (ie if he was thought to be still alive and was not a child at the time or of such a great age that whatever children there were would not have seemed highly unlikely). If so, the marriage card was placed beneath his baptism card and, if the next John could also have married at that time, beneath both of them. Thus we now knew that signature D, for example, belonged to either the John Smith baptized in 1738, or the one baptized in 1744. Using this method, we worked our way through the rest of the marriages and the Corndealer was found to have married twice and to have been named in a bond, wherein his brother stood guarantor. As his was the only signature amongst the marriages which was duplicated, this meant that no one else had married twice. We then tried to place any of the burials which were definite, such as those in which the age given was in agreement with one of the baptisms. Admittedly we had tried all of this once before and it had proved inconclusive, but now that we had the signatures, we could take it one step further. For we had also acquired the signatures, or marks, of any John Smiths who had witnessed a wedding or any other document and if one of those matched signature D, for example, we knew that the one who had married Mary Walker had witnessed the wedding etc. in 1780. That meant that he was still alive then and that none of the earlier burials could therefore be allocated to him. Alternatively, if the marriage in 1780 was that of a close relative of a John Smith, that told us which of them had married Mary Walker. To give an example, the marriage of William Smith of Towersey in 1776, had been witnessed by a John Smith who could not write and had therefore put his mark. We consulted the Towersey little Smith family tree and saw who this William was, and that he had a brother, John. The chances of another John Smith having witnessed his wedding, rather than his own brother, were negligible, as that would have been too much of a coincidence, which meant that the John Smith baptized 1747 in Towersey could not write. Thus, returning to the baptisms and marriages set out on the table before us, we saw that one of his possible marriages had a signature. That could not therefore be his marriage and was thus put with the other possibility, or possibilities. Whereas the one with the mark which had taken place in Sydenham and was not therefore the obvious choice, was given to him. This having thus enabled us to see who was alive and when, it helped us to place more of the burials and as more marriages and burials were allocated by this means, the field began to clear, leaving only John Smith baptized 1745 Chinnor, Oxfordshire and John Smith baptized 1738 Princes Risborough, Buckinghamshire who could have married Ann Giles of Saunderton in 1764 or Mary Darvill of Bledlow in 1768. Both of the bridegrooms had a signature, but as the marriages had taken place within a few years of each other, it was difficult to find some determining factor. As with 'Old Edward' and the trauma over the other Edward, aged ninety-one, in Buckingham, we were so close to success that we felt thoroughly deflated. We had done all that to find our John, but it had come to nothing.

It was, however, my birthday and where better to spend a birthday than in a Record Office? If you are anything like me anyway. Consequently, we set off for the Centre for Buckinghamshire Studies, with the intention of looking through more documents, in the hope that something might come of it. The John whom we had once thought would turn out to be ours, had been ruled out after our last visit, as he had been named in a settlement certificate along with his wife and child, when going from Princes Risborough to Monks Risborough. The document had made it clear who he was and, with this in mind, we decided to start by looking at more settlement certificates, as Angela had spotted a William Smith Jun. in the list provided by the Buckinghamshire Family History Society, going from Chinnor to Amersham in 1767. We were, of course, hoping that he was some relation of one of the Johns with whom we were left, and that he might thus throw some light upon the matter in hand. Whatever it was that I was looking at, whilst she was perusing the document is unimportant. For there was a sudden gasp and her little hand plunged into the folder into which we had put the family trees relating to all of the John Smiths. The document was referring to William Smith The Youngest and, once the Chinnor tree was before us, we saw at a glance why he was so named. As his Grandfather, referred to in the parish register as William The Elder, and his Father, William The Younger, were both still alive and he was indeed the youngest of three William Smiths. But, more importantly, he was the elder brother of the 1745 John Smith of Chinnor! – and even more importantly, this John was standing guarantor for him!!! There at the foot of the page was

John's signature, but we had not brought our copies of the signatures! The request form was filled out in great haste and the staff were just as quick to respond, yet how long those minutes seemed before the Saunderton parish register lay before us. Neither of us said a word. In the quietude of the search room, all that could be heard was that little hand carefully turning the pages, until Angela came at last to the marriage entry of John Smith and Ann Giles. The settlement certificate was placed beside it .... and what a birthday present! There he was – my Great Great Great Great Grandfather, John son of William and Mary Smith of Chinnor .... Oxfordshire ....

*Loosley Row, Buckinghamshire, as it would have been when
Jeptha Smith was living there or thereabouts
from 1841 to 1891.*

*The Buckinghamshire village of Bradenham,
remembered still in Surrey.*

7

Wheelwrights

It came as no surprise to find that my four-times Great Grandfather was the son of a William. For almost without exception, the eldest son was named for his paternal Grandfather during the 18th century and earlier and we had been hoping that it was in keeping with this that John and Ann of Saunderton Lee had called their first male child William. Some people occasionally broke with tradition, but since seven of their other nine children were named for themselves and/or members of her family, that did not seem to be the case. For even if he had quarrelled with his father and, because of bad feeling between them, had chosen a different name for his first son, it would surely have been that of her father, Richard. Until then, the only William that we had come across was one of her uncles on her mother's side, and to have named the child for him would have given him precedence over her father and would thus have caused even more bad feeling. We did not, however, allow this to influence us when trying to work out which John was the right one, but once we knew who he was, it was interesting to note that the names of their other two children which we had been unable to place, had turned out to be those of his mother and younger brother.

But how would we fare with a name like Smith in Chinnor? For whilst nowhere near as densely populated as it is now, it was nevertheless so much bigger than Saunderton Lee. There was, however, some hope. For a telephone call to the Oxfordshire Record Office, had resulted in a long list of documents relating thereto and we already knew, from having compiled the little family trees whilst searching for John (who went to Saunderton Lee), that there was only one other family of Smiths there at that time. They were descended from an Aaron, who had come into the parish in about 1744 and, thankfully, their only William was not born until 1753, whereas we had one in every generation and it was this which singled our family out. In order to make it clear to which of these Williams we are referring hereafter, they are as follows:-

Old William – No baptism or marriage in Chinnor. Buried 1700.

William The Elder (1680/1–1770) – Son of 'Old William'. Grandfather of John who went to Saunderton Lee. Became known to us as '*The Loving Brother*'.

William The Younger (1704–1770) – Son of 'William The Elder'. Father of John who went to Saunderton Lee.

William The Youngest (1739/40–1810) – Son of 'William The Younger'. Elder brother of John who went to Saunderton Lee. Went to Amersham in 1767.

Shown above are two examples of the way in which the year was written prior to 1752, when referring to a date between 1st January and 24th March. This is because the calendar changed from Julian to Gregorian in 1752 and whereas until then the year had begun on 25th March, thereafter it began on 1st January. Consequently, the baptism of William the Elder, for example, is written as 3rd March 1680/1, as at that time 3rd March was towards the end of the year 1680, but we now think of that date as what should have been 1681.

Returning however, to the aforementioned William

Smiths, we already knew something about them, as our previous search for the parentage of the John Smith, later of Saunderton Lee, had included delving into the background of all those who were possibilities, in the hope of finding some clue. Thus referring to them in reverse order, as we were of course working our way backwards, William the Youngest (1739/40–1810) played a fleeting yet vital part in our family history, in that his relocation to Amersham in 1767, provided us with the signature of his brother, John, on a settlement certificate, without which our search would have come to an end. We were hoping to find out more about him and therefore took advantage of a service provided by the Buckinghamshire Family History Society, whereby two hours research was undertaken per annum on behalf of out-of-county members. This enabled us to have digital photographs taken of the signatures and/or marks of every William Smith in Amersham, at the time when William the Youngest was there. We had made a list of these, including the dates of all relevant marriages etc., in order that the researcher had only to find the correct entry in the parish register, rather than search for it. The results were excellent and these we intended to compare with his signature on the settlement certificate, but in the midst of this project, our line of descent began gathering momentum in Chinnor and this had thus to be left in abeyance. However, we did discover that he had married in Amersham in 1766, which suggests that he had gone there to look for work. Had he remained single, he would have been allowed to reside in the parish for up to a year, whereas, once married he had had to return to Chinnor as both he and his wife were then chargeable to his parish if the need arose for Poor Relief. Presumably she was unhappy there, which was why they obtained a settlement certificate and went back to Amersham. Consequently, it was lucky for us that he fell in love with Mary Carpenter, or he may just have gone home once the year was up and no one would ever have known who his brother was.

The marriage of his parents, William the Younger and Mary Browne of Chinnor, took place 21st October 1731, at St Mary Magdalen in the City of Oxford, a little church renowned for clandestine marriages. Whether they eloped, we shall never know, but the likelihood certainly leads one to imagine a horseman tearing through the night with a pretty maid riding pillion, her head turned backwards in fear of pursuit! Were it so, the parents no doubt relented once the knot was tied and a son named for his father and grandfather was born in January 1732/3. Sadly he died, as did another four of their ten children and, when recording this, we were interested to see that the same names had been persistently chosen. For there were two Williams, two Anns and a Mary, two Johns and three Edwards. Some were the names of the parents and grandparents, but why was this William so determined upon a John and an Edward? The answer to that question lay hidden within the family tree and it was thus a while before it came to light. But we now know that those were the names of his Great Grandfathers on both sides of the family and that they were, in fact, the only male names in our direct line, other than William, as far back as our research has taken us.

At this stage though, we had only got as far as William the Elder (1680/1–1770), the son of 'Old William'. For although his family tree and that of his brother, John (1672–1757), had already been compiled, as part of the background information, during the search for John Smith, later of Saunderton Lee, we had yet to find a clue to their father's past as the parish register showed only his burial and gave no details. Yet rich in other information, it had now furnished us with a sturdy branch of the family tree in Oxfordshire. William the Elder had married Ann Brookes, of the nearby parish of Henton, in 1703 and their children were William (1704), Ann (1706), John (1708), Edward (1711/2), Elizabeth (1714), George (1716/7) and Mary (1718), whilst his brother, John, had married Ann Costard in 1698 and the tree now showed the baptisms (and burials of all but three) of their fifteen children. 'Old William' also had two daughters, one of whom married Jonathan Beckley, a Weaver, in 1703. Most clothing was then made from wool, which had to be woven into cloth, and as this was thus a lucrative occupation, the marriage would therefore have been considered a good match. By referring to the description of the Beckley premises, contained in an inventory, and to the contents of a will, we were able to assess Jonathan's status and this was also apparent from the fact that his Grandfather, Thomas Beckley, was one of the few people in Chinnor to have had a trade token. During a visit to the local library, we chanced upon an article on this subject, written by the Chinnor Historical and Archaeological Society, from which we learnt that brass or copper tokens to the value of a penny, a halfpenny, or a farthing, (which were, of course, worth very much more at that time) were issued by reputable tradesmen and honoured by those in the neighbourhood.

An interest in the layout of the 18th century village of Chinnor was stirring and, upon becoming members of the Chinnor Historical and Archaeological Society we were thus pleased to receive a copy of the pre-enclosure map, showing the strips of land in the common fields. This was later put to use when compiling a map of our own, based on which buildings were there at the time in which we were interested, but as yet we were still only wondering about the whereabouts of the long-ago weaver's shop, above which Jonathan and Letitia had resided. For we then had but one thought in mind – to find a clue to where 'Old William' (the father of William the Elder, John, Elizabeth and Letitia) had come from. We did not expect to discover anything more about his children. We knew who they were and that was that. Or so we thought .... But whilst trying to find the key to his past, we stumbled across something rather surprising. Signatures had, of course, been our first thought when looking for a clue, as they were the means by which we had managed to get that far. However, in this instance, we had no signature to compare and had thus to find one. The staff of the Oxfordshire Record Office very kindly brought us dozens of Chinnor wills and inventories, dated 1670 (as 'Old William's' first child was baptized 1672 and he was therefore known to have been there by then) – 1770 (the year in which William the Elder was buried), as we had decided to check not only for the signature of 'Old William', but also for those of his sons, John and William, in the hope that a will witnessed by one of them might contain some reference to our family and perhaps even that vital clue. It was indeed a faint hope and we did not seem to be making any progress. For at the end of the lengthy task, the early wills had yielded nothing and although the brothers had taken the inventory of Christopher Bigg, Wheelwright, in 1703, John had witnessed the will of Mary Bigg, mother of Christopher, in 1698 and William had taken the inventory of Dorothy Costard in 1727, these told us nothing. However, it was such a thrill to see their signatures thereon and although we did not know it at the time, all that somewhat tedious and time-consuming work was in fact a stepping-stone to success. For heartened by those mere mentions of our family, Angela went over to the personal name index in search of anything which might contain some further mention of them and came across a reference to a probate in the name of John Smith of Chinnor, Wheelwright. A request form was filled out for this, amongst other documents, and what a surprise! Beautifully written in old copperplate handwriting on parchment half the size of our dining-room table, it was such an important looking document, that somehow or other we never really thought that it could be anything to do with our family. For up until this point, they had been mostly agricultural labourers. Within the first few sentences however, he had left a bequest to his *loving brother William'* of:

'.... my messuage or tenement wherein my sister Elizabeth Keene widow deceased did lately dwell situate standing and being in Chinnor aforesaid and also all that my newly erected cottage or tenement wherein my nephew George Smith now dwells .... near to the said messuage .... and also .... my close of arable land .... called .... Pages containing by estimation one acre .... all which said premises late were the estate of my said sister Elizabeth Keene.'

And although, as we have already said, there were by this time other Smiths in Chinnor, the only William to whom this could apply was ours. The one in the document had to be William the Elder, hence the term 'the Loving Brother', used when referring to him thereafter, and the testator was obviously his elder brother, John (baptized 1672). Almost every other word was a feast of information! John's children were named, as were his sons-in-law and grandchildren and, as we read on, we learnt that 'the Loving Brother' was also a Wheelwright, an important profession in the 18th century. For there were no cars, no buses, no trains, not even a bicycle! People were dependant upon the horse and the wheel, for their carts, farm wagons, carriages, even their ploughs! There were no signatures on the document, but at the foot of an indenture dated 1765, which was included in a series of related documents, to which we shall refer later in the chapter, was the signature of 'the Loving Brother', in a rather courtly hand, together with his seal, which resembled the profile of a Roman with a beard, looking to the left. He must have worn a ring with this image upon it and, when signing his name, pressed it into the wax, making an impression which had lasted nearly 250 years!

The Elizabeth Keene referred to in the probate, turned out to be John and William's ('the Loving Brother') eldest sister, who had married William Keene of Sydenham, a relative of those who had inhabited Keene's Farm, which later became Hill Farm, at the Bledlow Ridge end of the village. Simply by chance, we came across a will (made 1755) at The National Archives long after this, in which Elizabeth names all of her brothers' and sister's children and from which we discovered that she had left the messuage, cottage and close called Pages, which she had received as part of a marriage settlement, to her two brothers, which was presumably why John then left it in entirety to William. At the age of seventy-six, he travelled to London to prove the wills of his brother and sister, which inasmuch as journeys were then hazardous and gentlemen were advised to carry firearms for protection against highwaymen, gives us some insight into his strength of character.

We had now begun to wonder about the possibility of other documents relating to our family and therefore checked the Oxfordshire Wills List 1733–1857. None of the innumerable Smiths were recognisable though, which was somewhat disappointing, but then under Beckley we found a reference for Letitia (1678/9–1727/8), widow of Jonathan and sister of John and William Smith ('The Loving Brother'). The date was 1728, at which time only a widow or a spinster was entitled to make a will, as a woman's property passed to her husband upon marriage. Her long list of bequests included a silver christening dish, two gold rings, a tester bed with curtains and, to son, John, *'two pewter dishes that are marked with his father's name'*, all of which are an indication of a good standard of living. Neither Letitia nor her husband had an inventory, but fortunately his father was also a weaver and would thus have shared the same premises and, having now begun our study of the village, the moment we read his inventory, dated 1716, we felt sure that it referred to the 17th century building with a Georgian facade, once known as London House, which is situated about halfway along the High Street. By comparing the layout of the rooms listed therein, with the plans and surveys on the South Oxfordshire District Council website, we were able to confirm this. It seems therefore, that not long after it was the scene of a skirmish between Cavaliers and Roundheads during the English Civil War, the Beckley looms began working within those walls, to provide woollen cloth for the community and continued to do so throughout the early part of the 18th century.

By this time, our interest in the layout of 18th century Chinnor, had been furthered by the bequest of *'the tenement or messuage .... and the close called Pages'*, and we were now intent upon finding out where it was. We had visited Chinnor on several occasions and had taken photographs of the oldest buildings, most of which seemed, at first glance, to date from the Georgian era. When seen from another angle however, such as from the side, or from behind, some were quite clearly of an earlier period and had had a Georgian facade added when that style of architecture became fashionable, perhaps as the owner could not afford the cost of rebuilding his property. Intrigued by the thought of history hidden beneath the surface of the village, we decided to compile a map, showing how it was at the time that our family were living there. Any buildings from before 1700 (the time of 'Old William') were to be coloured in red, those from 1700–1770 (during the adult life of 'the Loving Brother' and the lifetime of William the Younger) in yellow and those thereafter, until the time of the tythe map (1770–1844) in mauve. Anything after that time was to be omitted. Around the edges of the village, we would show the common fields, including the names of anyone who owned strips of land therein before Enclosure and if able to determine who owned which close etc., that too would be shown. The Ordnance Survey map dated 1900 (surveyed 1897) was the basis for this, as the buildings were then shown.

A large-scale sketch-map was made of the layout of the streets, the buildings and any other features, such as ponds, which may have been there in earlier centuries. This was then taken on several walks around the village, along with an excellent publication entitled, *'Chinnor in Camera'* (Mary Darmody-Cadle and Pat Whelehan), which was recommended to us by someone in the church whilst photographing the font at which William the Elder and Younger and John, later of Saunderton Lee, were baptized. It served as a guide as to which buildings were where and was particularly helpful in that the photographs were arranged in order of perambulation. Each building was studied in depth, the approximate age noted on our map, together with any relevant details, or if it had gone and/or had been replaced, the plot was marked accordingly.

Occupants sometimes volunteered information without which we may have made an incorrect assumption and for which we were therefore most grateful. For example, one gentleman, when asked whether his house was on the site of a centuries-old farmhouse, revealed that it *was* the farmhouse with a new skin of bricks around it! Also useful in determining the age of some properties were the plans, surveys and list descriptions on the South Oxfordshire District Council website and by comparing our map with the tythe map, which is precise as to the shape of each building and was thus a great help to us, we were able to tell whether we were looking at the one which was there at that time, or whether it had since been replaced or extended. This also enabled us to establish which properties were built before 1844 and erase those which were of a later date.

As our map began to take shape, we were to see the village not as it was, but as it once had been. Marked thereon were the premises of an earlier wheelwright, Christopher Bigg, whose inventory in 1703 was taken by John Smith (1672) and 'the Loving Brother'. This suggests that they were his apprentices and it seems likely that they set up in business on their own after his death. The will of his mother, Mary Bigg, proved in 1719, told us that the Bigg property was divided between her family, which means that John and William Smith would have had to have found some other premises and we were hoping to discover where. As their father, 'Old William', had died in 1700, John, being the eldest son, would by this time have inherited the property described in the probate dated 1757 as *'my Messuage Cottage or Tenement wherein I now dwell and the shop garden and hereditments'*. Although the wheelwright's shop may not have been included, (we have not yet proved that 'Old William' was a wheelwright), and the brothers may thus have turned part of the property into one when starting their own business. Could we find the place? We had already found the location of the other property referred to in the probate, as further searches of the name index and of any other relevant card indexes, had provided us with a series of documents with consecutive reference numbers to that which, when put together, had told us the whereabouts of the messuage, cottage and close called Pages, and even its history. In October 1643, Clement Surman, a carpenter, purchased the messuage, which he had recently built on land owned by Jeffrey Stevens, together with a barn and a close of meadow ground measuring approximately one acre. Within four years the barn had gone and a garden and orchard had been planted. The property changed hands several times, before William and Elizabeth Keene purchased it in 1736, as part of a marriage settlement. By this time, William Bishop Senior, the son-in-law of John Smith the Wheelwright (1672), had built another cottage on the plot and this was included in the purchase. As previously mentioned, Elizabeth Keene bequeathed the 'messuage' in which she had dwelt, the cottage occupied by her nephew, George Smith, and the close called 'Pages', to her brothers, John and William Smith, the Wheelwrights, and John subsequently left this in entirety to his *'loving brother'*, William. The records also show that George then purchased the cottage from his father, 'the Loving Brother', in 1765 and was still in occupation in 1785, at which time his son, Edward, was occupying the field attached thereto. Whether they were working there, or were simply using the field as a place to store seasoned wood and house some of the carriages and farm wagons awaiting repair, we have yet to find out. Before long though, both died within a year of each other and the 'Pages' property passed on to the other son, Thomas, a shopkeeper, and was subsequently sold to Buckinghamshire graziers, John and Thomas Smith. Relatives perhaps. (Whilst looking on the Access2Archives website for something quite different, we recently chanced upon a reference to a document held by the Hampshire Record Office, which was listed under the name of Stevens. A telephone enquiry resulted in a digital copy on CD and, to our surprise, we found that the close called 'Pages' was a part of the land purchased from Sir John Bulkeley of Southampton, in 1591. Thus the history goes on and we hope to follow this up still further in Hampshire.)

Every one of the transactions recorded in the series of documents with consecutive reference numbers, described where the messuage, cottage and close were situated, by referring to the surroundings. For example, '.... *adjoining the tenement and backside of Nicholas Butler on the south, the tenement and backside of Robert Howlett on the north, a close of Clement Surman on the west and the street of Chinnor on the east'*, and by applying this to our map, we had been able to work out a few possibilities. The choice was narrowed down by the fact that there had to be at least two buildings on the plot and with a little more information gleaned from the plans, surveys and list descriptions on the South Oxfordshire District Council website and from the wills and inventories of some of those thought to have been living in that part of the village, we had finally come to a conclusion.

The visit to Chinnor to see the 'Pages' property, was postponed however, as the tythe award used in conjunction with the 1841 Census, had enabled us to discover the names and occupations of those in each household and we were therefore hoping that this would lead us to the other property referred to in the probate. For if there were any discrepancies between the two, the answer was to be found in the burial register. This was thus a means of establishing the whereabouts of the village wheelwright's shop at that time and we were pinning our hopes on the fact that this John Fletcher's father, William Fletcher, was also a wheelwright and was old enough to have been apprenticed to those in our family. By looking for the name of Fletcher in the index of the parish register transcript, we came across entries which told us that William had a brother, another wheelwright, who was a lot older and could thus have been trained by 'the Loving Brother' and fully qualified by the time that the latter died. It therefore seemed likely that, when almost a century – and perhaps even longer than that – of Smith wheelwrights came to an end, with the untimely death of Edward Smith in 1789, at the early age of thirty, and that of his father, George, shortly afterwards, the Fletchers had stepped into their shoes and had perhaps taken over the premises as well as the business. This was why the site occupied by John Fletcher, the wheelwright in 1841, had become of interest, as this could well have been the other property referred to in the probate. For there cannot have been many places which fitted a wheelwright's requirements, inasmuch as he had need of somewhere with a wide frontage, that the great farm wagons might be brought in to await repair, preferably situated at the junction of two roads, in order to attract the most custom and if the Smiths had had just such a place, to which people from all around were accustomed to come, why bother to set up in business elsewhere?

We knew, of course, that the premises in which the brothers, John and William Smith, were plying their trade, were bequeathed to John's grandson, William Bishop, in 1757, but as he was a labourer, he would have had no use for a wheelwright's shop. Moreover, the Land Tax, which has survived for Chinnor from 1786–1832 (with a few gaps), shows that he had disposed of the property by 1786, as he is not listed, and as the parish register records his death in 1810 and those of his wife and daughter, who had predeceased him, he must have been in rented accommodation. Had he then sold the property to 'the

Loving Brother', who is likely to have been working with his son, George, throughout the remaining thirteen years of his life, and encouraging his grandson, Edward, to follow in their footsteps? Certainly 'the Loving Brother' took out a mortgage on 'Pages' in 1765 and was therefore trying to raise money for some purpose. Was it to purchase his father's house and wheelwright's shop, which had passed to his elder brother, rather than allow it to be sold away from the family? Or had William Bishop leased the property to him and subsequently to his son, George, and had the Fletchers then taken over the business and thus the premises by the time that George died? Again the Land Tax was useful, in showing that John Fletcher (Senior) was the owner of the property which had subsequently passed to the younger John Fletcher, the wheelwright at the time of the 1841 Census, by 1786. But there was, of course, one all-important question. Had it been handed down through his family? The only will which could throw any light on this, was that of the earlier John Fletcher, which was proved in 1820 and told us that he had bequeathed it to his brother and to his nephew, the 1841 wheelwright, at which time it was divided into two cottages. The fact that in the Land Tax exoneration certificate of 1799 it was described as *'a messuage'*, shows that it had been divided between that date and 1820. Again we turned to the parish register and found that there were no Fletcher baptisms prior to that of this earlier John Fletcher in 1746, nor were there any marriage or burial entries relating to them prior to that, which suggests that they came into the parish at around that time. This John Fletcher would have been approaching the age to begin an apprenticeship when John Smith, wheelwright, died in 1757, leaving his seventy-six-year-old 'Loving Brother' to carry on the business. For there were no pensions and therefore no retirement. The boy's father may thus have foreseen more than just a means of employment ahead and purchased the premises with that in mind.

We compared the description given in the probate with that in the tythe award and although at first glance they appeared to differ, in that the one referred to a messuage/ cottage/tenement, a shop and a garden, left by John Smith and the other to a *'house, buildings and garden'* owned by John Fletcher, the wheelwright in the 1841 Census, the *'buildings'* must have included a wheelwright's shop, as that was the latter's trade. The descriptions therefore matched and moreover, the location seemed significant in that it had turned out to be next door to Keene's Farm and the Smith property had been handed down from 'Old William', whose eldest daughter married a relative of the Keenes. Perhaps also significant was its proximity to the probable site of the long-ago manor house of Edward Stevens, the relevance of which will become clear later in the chapter.

In Oxfordshire again, in search of the Chinnor of old, we came first to the *'messuage, cottage and close called Pages'*, and tried to envisage how it once was. But the scene had changed beyond recognition. Only by checking the map could we be sure that we had the right place. For the *'messuage'*, having been extended in both directions, was only just discernible, whilst the close had become the garden and that of a newly-built bungalow in nearby Grafton Orchard. But at least by knowing this, we were able to judge the length of the plot and the minimum width during the 18th century was shown by the distance between the two cottages. For there to our right was the one built about 1736, an old, stone cottage now sandwiched between more modern buildings, yet still retaining its ancient charm.

Though saddened by the changes, our thoughts were treading paths long gone, as we made our way to what was once an old farm track at the junction of the High Street and Church Road, both no more than just muddy packways in earlier centuries. The track became known as Keene's Lane, as it led to Keene's Farm, the home of the family into which 'Old William's' eldest daughter married and there, but a stone's throw from the farmhouse, was the timber-framed house in which she would then have been living, if indeed 'Old William' had occupied the premises later occupied by John Fletcher, the wheelwright in the 1841 Census. This fine example of 17th century architecture, in a beautiful setting shaded by ancient chestnuts, was not much further from (what is now the site of) her maternal Great Grandfather's manor house, wherein her mother may have resided before marriage. Although, as the research which was to confirm this had not yet been completed, we were thinking only of wheelwrights at work there. For one could almost hear the great farm wagons trundling in through the one five-bar gate to await repair and out through the other once the job was done. The site of that gate is now in the adjacent plot, but the tythe map had shown that the barn, also in that plot yet right there beside the timber-framed house, could once have belonged to the property and that, in the absence of the Victorian cottages, since built in the forefront of the two, the wide frontage characteristic of a wheelwright's premises, may therefore have been wider still.

Though stood at the gate, admiring the charm of a bygone age, we had only just noticed the delicate design of oak leaves intertwined with Tudor roses, carved into the ancient wood of the gatepost. Grey with age and thus evocative of times gone by, it was a reminder that by such means would a carpenter once have advertised his trade. For at a time when carving on furniture, beams and joinery was a sign of status and therefore in demand, how better than to let passers-by see an example of his craftsmanship at the entrance to his property? Of course, we do not know for certain if 'Old William' was a carpenter as, we have since discovered, were his brother and a number of others in the family, or whether in fact he had started out as one and later became a wheelwright. But as I stood there, I somehow felt that that was the work of a Smith hand. For centuries later,

I had seen many an example of that same skill – the work of my father's hand .... It also occurred to me that, being from further afield, 'Old William' may have hoped that someone might one day come in search of him and might thereby see where he had put down roots. If so, that hope has at last been realised and we have found the tree from which those roots had sprung.

The search had already begun. The Chinnor parish records contained few references to him – only the baptisms of his children, his burial on 1st September 1700 and, in the Church Warden's accounts, a brief mention of the fact that he had forgotten to pay his contribution to the Poor Rate in 1683! (The fact that he was contributing to 'the Rate', as it was called, is a clue to his status, in that only those who could afford to do so, were expected to.) There was no marriage though and we were thus hopeful that this had taken place in the parish whence he had come, but in order to find it, we had had to know his wife's Christian name. No help could be gleaned from the baptismal entries of his children – John 12th June 1672, Elizabeth 25th February 1674/5, Letitia 1st January 1678/9 and William 3rd March 1680/1 – as we were now back to the time when only the father's name was given in the parish register. We had thus turned to the burial register and how fortunate we were that until 1744, there were no other Smiths in Chinnor. For therein we found a vital clue! The burial of an Elizabeth Smith widow 14th June 1735, who had to be the widow of 'Old William'. For who else could she be? His sons and their wives were still alive and there were no other burials for anyone who could have been his wife or her husband. Moreover his eldest daughter was named Elizabeth. We were surprised at the time that his widow had lived to such a great age, but have since found evidence that, contrary to belief, very many people were living until well into their eighties and some into their nineties in this part of Oxfordshire during the 17th century – 18th century. In fact, one woman in a nearby parish reached the age of 108!

Having thus established that 'Old William' had married an Elizabeth, we referred to the Oxfordshire Marriage Index and, as is again illustrated in Chapter 8, found the databases compiled by the Oxfordshire Family History Society just as useful as those compiled by the Buckinghamshire Family History Society. In fact, without such databases, our search would have got no further than Thomas and Dinah in Surrey. For with a name like Smith, we had to have the whole of the field set out before us, in order to be sure of our findings. In this instance, the Buckinghamshire and Berkshire marriage indexes also had to be checked, as Chinnor is so close to the borders of those two counties, and the overall search resulted in eight possible marriages, which were as follows:

1. William Smith of Oxford St Peter in the East and Elizabeth Tomy of Weston-on-the-Green, 9th February 1672/3 at Oxford St Cross, Oxfordshire.

2. William Smith and Elizabeth Stevens, 8th January 1670/1 at Chalgrove, Oxfordshire.

3. William Smith and Elizabeth Browne of Ickford, 2nd February 1670/1 at Thame, Oxfordshire.

4. William Smith and Elizabeth Burgess, both of Charlton-on-Otmoor, 7th October 1668 at Oxford St Peter Bailey, Oxfordshire.

5. William Smith of North Leigh and Elizabeth Baxter of Finstock, 4th February 1659/60 at Woodstock, Oxfordshire.

6. William Smith of Cuxham and Elizabeth Wise of Hambleden, Buckinghamshire, 5th May 1656 at Watlington, Oxfordshire.

7. William Smith and Elizabeth Steevenes both of the parish of Great Marlow, 19th October 1668 at Great Marlow, Buckinghamshire.

8. William Smith and Elizabeth Symones, 8th February 1663/4 at Stony Stratford, Buckinghamshire.

The time span was a thirty year period prior to the birth of the last child, to allow for Elizabeth to have married at a very early age, which the law then allowed. For although their known children were baptized from 1672–1681, in Chinnor, there could have been others prior to that in some other parish. All of the aforementioned couples had to be followed up in any relevant parishes, in the hope of finding a burial there and/or the baptisms of children after 1672, as 'Old William' and his Elizabeth were then known to have been in Chinnor and that couple could therefore be ruled out. This was not quite as straightforward as we had hoped, inasmuch as we had sometimes had to check two or three parishes, instead of just one, if, for example, the Bride was from parish A, the Groom from parish B and they had married in the city of Oxford, as they could have remained there, or returned to either one of the other two parishes. It was thus a lengthy process and so much depended upon it, that there were some anxious moments towards the end. For the couple from Great Marlow had had no children and were thus reliant upon the burial entries, which were inconclusive. The problem was, that there was more than one William Smith in the parish who could have married the Elizabeth in question and, whilst it made no difference which one of them had done so, we had to be sure that the couple had remained in the parish. Family trees were compiled for each of the Williams there, as even the earlier ones, who already had wives and children, had to be included, as some of the burials related to them. These were therefore ruled out and we were left with two possibilities, neither of whom appeared, at first glance, to have had a burial. Yet there was a burial of an Elizabeth, wife of William Smith, in March 1723/4, which seemed to suggest that he was still alive. Was he then 'William Smith the Elder', buried in January 1726/7? It seemed unlikely, as the couple in whom we were interested, had had no children and there was a burial of a *'William Smith Junior'* in April 1722, who was thought to be the son of 'the Elder'. But there were no other possible burials .... Fortunately, William 'the Elder' had left a will and, though the copy was a long while coming – a long and anxious while – it was well worth the wait. For it showed that he had had no children and the bequests included a box belonging to his late wife, thereby confirming that this was the right couple and that they had indeed remained in Great Marlow.

This was our first brush with something which was rather confusing, but which, as time went on and we studied more documents and registers and became familiar with the use of certain terms, was proven in both Oxfordshire and Buckinghamshire and may therefore have occurred in other counties. For as well as applying the terms 'Senior' and 'the Elder' and 'Junior' and 'the Younger' to a father and son with the same Christian name, in some parishes during the 17th and 18th centuries, the vicar was differentiating between seemingly unrelated men with the same names by using such terms. For example, two Francis Quatermaines who were baptized only eighteen months apart, were known throughout their lives as 'Senior' and 'Junior' and in the same parish the John Quatermaines who were alive at the same time, were referred to as 'John Quatermaine the Elder at the Stone', 'John Quatermaine at the Stone', and 'John Quatermaine the Younger at the Stone', these being three generations of the same family, and 'John Quatermaine Senior' and 'John Quatermaine Junior', who were seemingly unrelated, the first being the elder of the two. Similarly a William Childe Senior and William Childe Junior, shown in a 17th century tenant list, were not related. In the Great Marlow case, the two William Smiths with whom we were left, though not father and son, were referred to in the burial register as 'the Elder' (baptized 1645) and 'Junior' (baptized 1648/9), and at the time, being unfamiliar with the use of these terms, we could only hazard a guess as to what the vicar was about!

Thankfully though, we were at last left with the one marriage, that of William Smith and Elizabeth Stevens in January 1670/1, at Chalgrove, which fitted with the baptism of 'Old William's' first child (John, the wheelwright) in June 1672. The evidence in support of this being the right marriage, has been set out as a comparison between 'Old William' and William Smith of Chalgrove and between our Elizabeth, (the wife of 'Old William'), Elizabeth Stevens of Chinnor and the Elizabeth Stevens who married William Smith at Chalgrove in 1670, in order to show that they were one and the same.

OLD WILLIAM	WILLIAM OF CHALGROVE
Married an Elizabeth	Married Elizabeth Stevens
Had 4 children	Had 4 children (see **ii** below)
Died September 1700	Died before March 1704/5 (see **i** below)
Wife outlived him	Wife outlived him (see **ii** below)
Children outlived him	Children outlived him (see **ii** below)
Not baptized in Chinnor	Born in Chalgrove
Not married in Chinnor	Married in Chalgrove
Died in Chinnor	Did not die in Chalgrove
Eldest son named John at time when usually named after father	Father named John

OUR ELIZABETH	ELIZABETH STEVENS OF CHINNOR	THE ELIZABETH STEVENS WHO MARRIED IN CHALGROVE
Married William Smith of Chalgrove (Old William)	Not married in Oxfordshire unless to William Smith	Married William Smith of Chalgrove
Had 4 children		Had 4 children
Was widowed in September 1700		Was widowed by March 1704/5
Children outlived their father		Children outlived their father
	Baptized in Chinnor	Not baptized in Chalgrove
Not married in Chinnor	Not married in Chinnor	Married in Chalgrove
Children born between 1672 and 1681	Born 1644 (therefore of child-bearing age between 1672 and 1681)	Married 1671 (fits with first child 1672)
Died in Chinnor	There were two Elizabeth Stevens – this Elizabeth and her niece – who did not marry in Chinnor, or anywhere else in Oxfordshire, other than Chalgrove (niece not old enough to do this), but only one died *single* in Chinnor	Did not die in Chalgrove
Eldest son named John		Husband's father named John
Daughter named Elizabeth	Mother named Elizabeth	
Daughter named Letitia (an uncommon name and no one in husband's family by that name)	Had a cousin named Letitia, (who may have grown up as her sister) (see **iii** below)	
	Father yeoman	Husband's father yeoman (same class)
Grandson named Edward (no Edwards known in family prior to that)	Father and brother named Edward	
	Family from Chinnor (brother and sister there). Her uncle, John Saywell, who may have acted as her guardian, was related to William of Chalgrove's mother and this uncle's mother was from Chalgrove and he had relatives there (see **iv** below)	Family not from Chalgrove (only one Stevens family there early in seventeenth century; they all died)

Some of the evidence shown in these comparison tables, came to light as time went on and our research broadened to include Chalgrove. Most importantly, William of Chalgrove's elder brother, John, who died in March 1704/5, left a monetary bequest *'to Elizabeth wife of my late brother William Smith deceased*(i) *and to her four children ....'*(ii) which confirms, firstly, that his brother had married an Elizabeth, whereas another William Smith in Chalgrove married Ann Overstricke in 1672/3 and lived well into the 1700s; secondly that William had four children (who outlived him); and thirdly that he had died by then and it was not as if he was so old that this was only to be expected. He can only have been in his fifties.

Elizabeth's father, Edward Stevens, Yeoman of Chinnor (1610–1647), also died young and named his *'brothers'*, James Stevens and John Saywell, as the overseers of his will. James Stevens was in Towersey and is therefore unlikely to have had much say in the upbringing of his brother's three young children, whereas John Saywell, who was married to his sister, Ann, lived nearby in Chinnor and may thus have acted as their guardian. If so, whilst he was keeping a watchful eye over them, his daughter, Letitia,(iii) and her cousin, Elizabeth Stevens, were likely to have been growing up as close as sisters, which would explain why that name was given to Elizabeth's younger daughter. A parish register entry and documents relating to Elizabeth's brother's children, show that John Saywell's close association with the family continued throughout the years. Indeed these children are known to have been living in his household after the death of their father in 1677. It therefore seems likely that he arranged Elizabeth's marriage, as was customary during the 17th century, as her other uncle, James Stevens, died in 1669. Or perhaps she met 'Old William' through him. For John Saywell had relatives in Chalgrove – his mother, formerly Lettice Burnham, was from there and her family were still in the village; his cousin, Michael Burnham, had married 'Old William's' cousin, Mary; and his father was related to 'Old

William's' mother, formerly Avis Quatermaine.**(iv)**

During the search for 'Old William's' roots, we researched the Stevens in Chinnor and some in Bledlow, using their wills to determine who was who and an article written by Peter Stevens, on the 'Stevens of Stanton, Horspath and Chinnor' and, in so doing, we came across something rather surprising. For this reason, they deserve a brief mention herein, as our discovery shows how interesting it can be, at times, to research the distaff side. For Elizabeth, the wife of 'Old William', was, as we have said, the daughter of Edward Stevens (1610–1647) and therefore the granddaughter of Edward Stevens (c.1564–1617), who was educated at Jesus College and Magdalen Hall, Oxford (1581–1585) and later became Vicar of Bledlow. Henry Stevens, the elder brother of this Edward, bought the manor of Bulkley's, in Chinnor, in 1591 and as he died without issue, left it to his brother, which means that our Elizabeth's grandfather became Lord of the Manor! This is another avenue which we have yet to explore, but at this stage in our research, our sights were set on 17th century Chalgrove ....

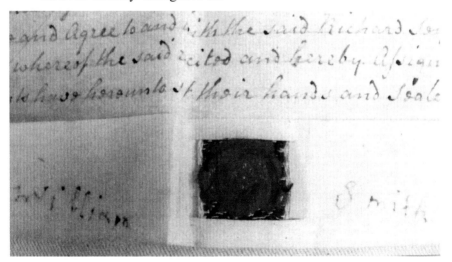

Signature and seal of William Smith, wheelwright of Chinnor,
('The Loving Brother') on an indenture dated 1765.
Reproduced by kind permission of Oxfordshire History Centre.

8

Yeoman and Freeholder

A battle took place in June 1643 at Chalgrove Field, between Prince Rupert's Horse and the pursuing Roundhead army. The Prince had led a surprise attack on Chinnor and was returning hotfoot to Oxford with over a hundred prisoners, but his efforts to reach the heavily guarded bridge at Chislehampton were thwarted by the captives dragging behind in the hope that their fellow Roundheads would catch up. A brilliant tactician, he thus decided to stand and fight when he came to a suitable location and the outcome was not only a triumph for the Royalists, but a further and far greater blow to the Roundhead cause, in that the leading Parliamentarian, John Hampden, was mortally wounded.

This was all that we knew of Chalgrove when we embarked upon the next stage of our research. Although, strangely enough, when a Fresher at St. John's College, Oxford, some years earlier, Angela had travelled there by bus in order to see the battlefield, not knowing that her family had actually been living there at the time!

I too have always been passionately interested in the English Civil War, but have to admit that when researching family history, it is, at the very least, a stumbling block. Already it had been the cause of another branch of the family being unable to reach back any further than 1684, and having now heard that Chalgrove was a Royalist Prebend and that the font had been hidden at Wallingford Castle for the duration of the war and perhaps even throughout most of the Interregnum, we were indeed apprehensive. The parish register is, without doubt, difficult to read. Moreover, there are gaps, one of them from 1642 (the start of the Civil War) – 1655, which was the very period during which 'Old William', having married in 1670, was likely to have been born. It therefore looked as if we were up against the very problem that I had encountered many years before.

One of the reasons for this widespread disruption of Church records, was that many people disapproved of the ecclesiastical changes made between 1645 and 1660 and therefore did not have their children baptized, unless in secret, and the introduction of a fee of one shilling (much more than it sounds today) was a further discouragement. The changes included laws passed in 1653–4, undermining the authority of the clergy and thereafter *'some able and honest person'*, known as *'the Parish Register'* (Registrar), made a note of any births and deaths (as opposed to baptisms and burials) in a book of some sort which probably did not survive. The aforementioned laws gave Justices of the Peace the right to marry a couple and those who disagreed with this either went to another parish which clung to the old ways, if not openly, or married in secret and, if this was written down, the record may have gone astray. Moreover, some records may have been lost, damaged or destroyed during the conflict, or the Vicar/Clerk may simply have forgotten to make the entry, due to the uncertainty of the times. However, having got that far with a name which we had never expected to be able to trace at all, we were not about to give up easily. We had to at least try. All Smith baptism, marriage and burial entries were therefore extracted from the parish register and we were relieved to see that again there were very few. As we had thought, no possible baptisms came to light for

141

'Old William', but there was a marriage of a John Smith[2] and Avis Quatermaine in 1639, which seemed to be the right sort of time, if their son had married in 1670. Moreover, 'Old William's' eldest son, who should have been named for his Grandfather, was John .... The baptisms of only two sons were recorded however. Any other children must have been born during the gap in the parish register and if 'Old William' was one of them, how were we ever to prove it?

It was indeed fortunate that amongst a jumble of articles cut from the pages of family history magazines, we came across a write-up of a talk, given by Michael Gandy, very aptly entitled, 'Wills – The Best Source There Is', and if he is reading this, we can never thank him enough. For it was this that pointed us in the right direction. References were found for two possible John Smiths in the Oxfordshire Wills List 1516–1732 and therein lay the proof that 'Old William' was the son of John Smith, Yeoman of Chalgrove. This has been set out in full in the previous chapter, but as much of it was found amongst the records pertaining to Chalgrove, this chapter would not be complete without some mention of it. Briefly therefore, a burial entry in the Chinnor parish register gave us the name of 'Old William's' wife and the Marriage Indexes yielded eight possible marriages. All but one were eliminated, leaving us with the marriage of William Smith and Elizabeth Stevens in Chalgrove in 1670. Elizabeth having been the daughter of Edward Stevens, yeoman of Chinnor and his wife, Elizabeth, this seemed to suggest that William was from Chalgrove, but because of the gap in the register at the time of the Civil War and Interregnum, he had no baptism. Thankfully though, in his will, dated 1676,

2 During the 1500s–1600s and earlier, spelling was not consistent and Y was more commonly used than I, these being interchangeable. Thus the same person/family could be variously referred to as Smith(e)/ Smyth(e) or Quatremain(e)/Quatremain(e)/Quatremayne/Quatremayne/ Catterman(n)/Katermain etc., sometimes even in one document. For the purpose of clarity, a single spelling has been used for each name throughout this chapter and the next, except when quoting from an original source.

John Smith the Elder, Yeoman of Chalgrove, named his five sons – John, George, Daniel, <u>William</u> and Robert and from this we learnt that William had married by then. Although, as we were new to this source, we were puzzled at first by the bequests of one shilling apiece to George, Daniel and William which denoted this. It was only as time went on and we read many more wills and became familiar with 17th century wording and procedure, that we came to know that it was then customary for a son or daughter to receive his/her portion at the time of marriage, whereupon any subsequent will would contain only a token bequest of one shilling, or some other such small sum. Reference is made to Daniel Smith's marriage settlement in his inventory, dated 1682, and it is clear from the will of his elder brother, George, that he too had been given his share which, in his case, included the part of the freehold property which was not bequeathed to the eldest, and at that time unmarried, son, John. (The purpose of a marriage settlement seems to have been to provide an income for the couple and/or for the widow, should the need arise.)

To continue however, with the proof that 'Old William' was the son of John and Avis Smith, we now knew that their son, William, had married by 1676, which fitted nicely with the fact that 'Old William' had married in 1670. <u>BUT</u> there was another marriage .... A William Smith had married Ann Overstricke in 1672 and if <u>he</u> was the son of John of Chalgrove, as we now called him, we would never know who 'Old William' was. Thus, hoping against hope, we turned to the other will located in the Oxfordshire Wills List, in search of further proof. As we became more familiar with this source, we found that the wills of those who were childless were often the most informative, inasmuch as they included bequests to other members of the family such as nieces, nephews and cousins, thereby determining relationships and background, and, thankfully, this was just such a will. In John Smith the younger's own words, '.... *I give to Elizabeth wife of my late brother William deceased and to her foure children ten shillings apeece ....'* He had thus told us that his brother, William, had died by 18th March 1704/5, had named his wife and had even said how many children he had and we knew, of course, that it was our 'Old William' who had married Elizabeth Stevens in Chalgrove in 1670 and that he had four children. One of the staff of the Oxfordshire Record Office told us that this was indeed proof enough. However, further evidence came our way as we broadened our search to include more wills. For, interestingly, Avis Smith, formerly Quatermaine, the mother of 'Old William', and John Saywell, the uncle and probable guardian of Elizabeth Stevens, were found to be related (second cousins) through their great grandmother, who, strangely enough, was also her paternal step-grandmother. Avis' mother was Elizabeth Symeon, the daughter of Richard Symeon of Golder (Pyrton), whose widowed mother, Joan Symeon, married John Quatermaine, the father of Avis' father, Daniel Quatermaine. This Joan had also had a daughter, Maude, (not a common name) who was living in Pyrton in 1583/4 and was single (will of Richard Symeon Senior). No record of her marriage has survived, nor is there a burial entry relating to Maude Symeon, yet she had died before 1625. There are other records however, which point to her having become the wife of Christopher Saywell (grandfather of the John who is thought to have arranged 'Old William's' marriage) and died in childbirth. For the Depositions made by Christopher Saywell of Chinnor and his son, John, tell us that Christopher was then in Pyrton and that John was born there in 1588, and there is an entry in the burial register which reads, *'4th November 1588, Maude, wife of Christopher Saywell'*. Obviously, this alone would be insufficient proof, but in her will, proved 1625, Joan Quatermaine, formerly Symeon, bequeathed sixty per cent of her money to *'John Saywell of Chinnor'* and his children, and left all of her land to him. All of the other bequests were to known members of her family, namely her son, Richard Symeon, three of her grandchildren coming from him and seven great grandchildren coming from him (including Avis

Quatermaine, who later married John Smith and became the mother of 'Old William'). Joan Quatermaine's son, Richard Symeon, had already inherited his father's land by the time that she made her will and she was effectively leaving her land to her deceased daughter, Maude. For John Saywell of Chinnor must have been a close relative to have received such a legacy, and who else could he have been but the son of Maude? Richard Symeon, having been under twenty in 1583/4, (will of Richard Symeon Senior) cannot have been his grandfather and we know that he was not his father. Maude was Joan's only other child. Another indication of this relationship is the fact that Richard Symeon had eleven children still living in 1625, yet only three of them received bequests, and even if she had not wanted to leave anything to the other eight, she would have left her land and most of her money to the three that she favoured, if not to her son, had she not had some other intention. Further proof lies in the fact that John Saywell had brothers and sisters, coming from Christopher's second wife, but they received nothing whatsoever, which shows that the connection between Joan Quatermaine and the Saywells was his first wife, Maude. John Saywell must therefore have been Joan's only grandchild coming from her daughter. This made the younger John Saywell, who later married Anne Stevens, the second cousin of Avis Smith (née Quatermaine), and explains why, when having become the guardian of his niece, Elizabeth Stevens, he found her a husband amongst his own family. The discovery of the relationship between John Saywell and Avis Smith, was therefore further proof of the link between 'Old William' and John and Avis Smith of Chalgrove, as was the marriage of John Saywell's cousin, Michael Burnham of Chalgrove, to 'Old William's' cousin.

The path had thus led from Chinnor to Chalgrove, but now that we were faced with another John Smith, was that where it would come to an end? .... I have to admit that we were none too confident. It had been hard enough the first time and we were now beyond the realms of signatures in the marriage register. But that said, we thought ourselves fortunate in that there was only one family of Smiths in the parish during the early part of the 17th century and we naturally assumed that they would turn out to be ours. However, although the marriage of John Smith and Christian Child was found in 1603 and the baptisms of their four children from 1604–1616, there was not a John amongst them .... It therefore looked as if we would never know who John of Chalgrove was .... but we could at least try to find out something about his life. For in addition to the will, dated 1676, there was also an inventory of his goods and chattels, taken on the day that he died, 14th April 1679, and as these were listed room by room, this told us the layout of his house. Fascinated, we wanted to know where it was and what it was like, and our foray into local history, which added so much colour and interest to our family history, was to have been included herein, but has grown to such vast proportions that it has had to be given separate cover. Briefly though, inspired by the thought that we might discover where in Chalgrove our family were living at that time, we embarked upon a study based on the Hearth Tax of 1662–6, made possible by the fact that the earliest return was written in the order that the village constables walked when compiling the list. It was however, much more complicated than we had expected and, in order to be sure of our findings, we had to refer to the manorial records held by Magdalen College, Oxford and Lincoln College, Oxford (the Lords of the Manors), the tithe map and tithe award, the Enclosure map, the Land Tax returns, wills and inventories from the 16th to the 19th centuries, and to the excellent publications produced by the Chalgrove Local History Group. As 'Friends' of the Group, we received a list of Smith references and another of those relating to the name of Quatermaine, both of which were to prove most useful, and have more recently been given some assistance in ascertaining the number of original hearths which some of the older houses have, as we thought at first that this would help us to accomplish this study.

The information gleaned from the aforementioned sources, was pieced together like a jigsaw puzzle and as a picture began to form, it was like reading a story, except that the characters were real people, some of whom had turned out to be distant relatives whom we may never otherwise have known about, whilst the setting was a now familiar place. The buildings came to mean more to us. For example, Fairleigh Cottage was now James Meades' house, which his father had acquired through marriage and The Red Lion was no longer a public house, but the home of Robert Quatermaine, the son of John the Butcher. The Green whereon the war memorial stands became Church Lane again and the long-ago Green was once more at the west end of what is now the High Street. Many such changes were beginning to unfold and it was as though we had found a door to the past and had somehow travelled back through time.

The manorial records are bursting with information, most of which refers to the many copyhold properties and provides a detailed account of ownership, inasmuch as the leases had to be renewed. There is no such record of the far fewer freehold properties, although the death of a Freeholder and the admission of his heir was usually noted. Not even the copyhold properties are named however. There is merely a description which is adhered to throughout the centuries and only changes if part of the property is sold. It was these descriptions which enabled us to trace the ownership of the majority of the houses, but in tracing the property owned by John of Chalgrove, we could expect no such help. Yet we must have had more than just luck. For once we had established his identity and knew for certain that he was the only John Smith, Freeholder, in the Lincoln College, Oxford, manorial records during the period in which we were interested, we came across an entry recording that the freehold land *'late Francis Quatermaine'* was *'sold to the said John Smyth'* in 1638 and a relief of two shillings and four pence had to be paid to the lord. *'.... the said John Smyth'* points to the fact that he was already a Lincoln tenant

147

and this is borne out by entries in the first Court Baron held after the sale, 24th June *'in the 17th year of the reign of King Charles'* (the First – 1641) which read *'John Smythe for land in Chalgrove late Francis Quatermayne'* and *'John Smythe for land in Roke'* and by earlier entries subsequently found in 1634 and 1626, which refer only to the Roke property (later inherited by his son – will of George Smith).

The previous owners of the Chalgrove property, were Richard Stevens, gent., Henry Stevens, gent., and John Edwards, gent., none of whom were from Chalgrove, but as the latter was the overseer of the will of William Quatermaine in 1640, (the inventory was taken by John of Chalgrove who, incidentally, was the overseer of William Quatermaine's wife's will), we saw from this that he was from Forest Hill, in Oxfordshire, and were thus able to find his will (made in May 1643) at The National Archives. Interestingly, it was one of several which we have come across during and shortly after the Civil War, which show that the testator was a Royalist, in this instance by the inclusion of the words, *'.... if theis daingerous tymes doe not amende by the setlement of a blessed peace both in Church and State under the goverment of our gracious Kinge ....'* Henry Stevens became Waggon-Master-General to King Charles I during the conflict, as is recorded in The Oxfordshire Record Society publication (Volume XLII) entitled *'The Papers of Captain Henry Stevens'*, and it is therefore likely that his father, Richard, who had married Anne Edwards, was also for the King. Consequently, the land passed from Royalists to Royalist! For John of Chalgrove is amongst those listed in *'Oxfordshire Contributors to the Free and Voluntary Present to King Charles II, 1661'*, (published by Oxfordshire Family History Society in association with The Family History Partnership), a record of a gesture which, after a nearly twenty year struggle to reinstate the monarchy, all true Royalists would have made, whether or not impoverished by the war. This is borne out by the fact that there were some who, judging by their occupations, could scarcely afford to contribute, yet clearly wanted to give <u>something</u>, whereas others, named in the Hearth Tax the very next year and known to have had ample means, are noticeably absent from the list. From another useful book, entitled, *'Politics and Loyalty in Post-Revolution Oxfordshire: The '1690' County Parliamentary Poll; The Association Oath Rolls, 1695–6'*, (published by Oxfordshire Family History Society in association with The Family History Partnership), we learnt that his son had voted Tory in the 1690 election. Only ten men were entitled to vote in Chalgrove, these being the Freeholders (to whom we shall refer later), which illustrates how few of them there were at that time.

It was this son, John, who inherited the property in 1679 and was formally admitted to it at the next Lincoln College Court Baron, held on 20th June 1681 – *'Item we present the death of John Smith of Challgrowe and do find a relife due to the lord of this maner 2s 4d and doe find John Smith his son to be the next eare'*. As he died without issue, it should then have passed to his younger brother, Robert, but in his will, proved 1704/5, he overrode his father's wishes and left everything to his wife, Joan, formerly Buckland, and by such means it passed out of the family.

The words, *'thear free hold'* and, (translated from the Latin), *'the freehold land late Francis Quatermaine'*, seemed to suggest that the property which was changing hands in 1638, was only land. Especially since earlier entries relating to this Francis Quatermaine, including the sale of his property in 1636 to the three *'gents'*, refer only to land. We therefore thought that John of Chalgrove had built a house upon it, as at the time that his son was admitted, it is described as a <u>messuage</u> and one and a half virgates. However, until later in the century, it must just have been common practise to record only the freehold land, irrespective of whether or not there was anything built upon it, as a further entry relating to this property, in a survey of the village, carried out by Magdalen College in 1551, refers to a *'tenement, close and backside'*, thus proving that there was already some sort of dwelling there then.

Which house was it though? We embarked upon the local

history project in the hope of finding out and after a few false starts, the pieces began to fall into place and suddenly we knew. Yet how were we to prove it? For it was freehold property and, as previously mentioned, the colleges did not keep any record of such. Joan Smith had inherited it from her late husband, John, son of John of Chalgrove, and seemed to have died intestate in 1725/6, so that, we thought, was that. But our luck held. We had set it aside and were busying ourselves with the numerous other houses, reading as many wills and inventories as we could find, that they, if not our own, would have the proof that they needed, and in amongst them was the will of Jeffrey Goode. Proved in 1745, it contained the words,

> '*Item I give devise and bequeath .... All that my Messuage or Tenement and Close thereto belonging and all other the premises which were lately given unto me by my late Aunt Joan Smith and lying and being in Chalgrove aforesaid .... In Trust .... during the naturall Life of my said Daughter Jane Wiggins .... the Rents Issues and Profitts of the said premises .... for her own Separate Use apart from her Husband so that he shall not intermeddle or have any thing to do with the said premises ....*'

At that time a wife's property became that of her husband, who could then have sold it. This was thus left in trust in order to safeguard it for the granddaughter.

> '*.... And from and imediately after the decease of my said Daughter Jane .... my said grandaughter Mary Wiggins and her Assigns to have hold and Enjoy the said premises .... for and during the Term of her naturall Life And from and imediately after her Decease Then .... to the Use of the Heirs of the Body of my said Grandaughter Mary Wiggins forever And in Default of such Issue of her Body Then to the use of my other two Grandaughters Mary White and Elizabeth Coles ....*'

Later, whilst looking through the Lincoln College manorial records, we came across an entry to the same effect, which read:

'We present the death of Joan Smith a freehold tenant since the last corte seased of on yeard land and halfe [ie one and a half virgates] *in Chalgrove within this mannar .... and Jeoffrey Good is the next eire and ought to be metted tenent.'*

(Interestingly, it looks as if John of Chalgrove was the only one holding freehold Lincoln property in Chalgrove, and the Tenant Lists 1638–1708 also give a clue to his status, in that he was at the head of the list of freeholders throughout his lifetime, as were his sons, George and John thereafter and, subsequently, this John's widow, the aforementioned Joan, and the tenant to whom George's son had sold his property, which was in Roke, in the place of George).

Returning, however, to Jeffrey Goode and to the relationship set down in his will, we saw from the little family trees which had been helping us with our research, that his mother was Mary Buckland, the eldest sister of Joan Buckland, who had married John of Chalgrove's son. Having had no children of her own, she had bequeathed the Smith property to her nephew and although her will had not survived, we had managed to find that out from his and we now knew that he had left it to his granddaughter. Hot on this unexpected trail, we turned to the Wiggins family tree, in search of Mary, and there she was, the daughter of George and Jane Wiggins, formerly Goode. But had she lived? Or had the property been divided between his other two granddaughters, Mary White and Elizabeth Coles? The Chalgrove parish register transcript having yielded no possible burial entries, her name was put into the marriage database and it brought up the very match for which we were searching, that of Mary Wiggins *'of Chalgrove'* and William Smith of Pyrton, in Pyrton in 1763. Their children were subsequently found –

Elizabeth in Chalgrove in 1764 and, in Pyrton in 1770 ....
a <u>JOHN SMITH</u>!!! That we should have come up against
that name again, and this time not even in our own family,
seemed rather unfair. However, somehow or other we had
to get as far as the Magdalen College survey of Chalgrove,
dated 1822, in order to have absolute proof of which house
it was. For therein, each property has been given a number
and these numbers are listed under the owner's name and can
be found on the accompanying map. The house or messuage
once owned by John of Chalgrove, was thus shown to have
been in the possession of John Newell, a Blacksmith from
Brightwell Baldwin, who bequeathed it to his infant son in
1836, but unless we could bridge the gap between this John
Newell and the 1798 Land Tax, which seemed to suggest that
John Smith had inherited the property from his mother, the
proof was incomplete. Almost in desperation, we scoured
both family trees, in search of something which would
explain why the one John had left this to the other and did,
in fact, find that they may have been distantly related, as
John Newell's sister, Jane, is thought to have married John
Smith's second cousin, but this did not seem a sufficient
reason for such a bequest and we therefore concluded that
it had been sold and that the bill of sale had not survived.
There was no more to be said. Our luck had held for nearly
100 years, yet for the sake of just another twenty-four, all
of our efforts had come to nothing. The study as a whole
had proved so fascinating though and so many of the other
houses now had a complete record, or were near completion,
that we soon became absorbed in trying to find out more
about those which had yet to finish and, during the course of
this, Angela remembered that she had read something useful
about the Land Tax. Until then, we had only referred to the
1798 assessment, held by The National Archives, but having
seen from a family history book that the County Record
Offices held a run of them, we studied those for Chalgrove
in depth from 1785–1832. It was a tremendous help to us
and the results are included in our local history project, but

the crowning point was the fact that this record of ownership covered the missing twenty-four years, and more besides, in respect of the property in which we were most interested. In 1785, it was owned by Mary Smith (formerly Wiggins). It passed to her son, John Smith, in 1791, which fits with the burial of a Mary Smith in Pyrton in 1788, as the Land Tax was often a little late in recording a change of ownership. This is verified by the fact that some of those listed, have a will proved some years earlier. By 1809 the property was in the possession of John Newell. Whether or not he purchased it, was of no importance, although he must have done so, as the two possible burials of John Smith are after that date. But all that mattered was that he was the owner. We now had no need of a bill of sale. It was there in black and white, the final piece of proof that the large, L-shaped farmhouse, at the eastern end of the village, later known as 'The Passage', was once the home of John of Chalgrove.

Sadly, our hopes of standing on the threshold were never realised, as it had been demolished in the 1960s, to make way for newer housing. There are photographs though and its memory lingers on in the words of Mr Ken Batley, President of the Chalgrove Local History Group, who once occupied one of the three cottages into which the house was divided during the early part of the 19th century. As we sat beside him, listening intently, it was as though we were on that threshold, looking in through the screens passage characteristic of a yeoman's house, at an old, oak-panelled room. We could almost hear the jangle of spurred boots echoing across the polished oak floorboards and feel the warmth from the inglenook fireplace, about which were 17th century implements.

'.... *In the Halle chimney* ....' Those were not the words of our new-found friend, but of others, who had walked from room to room in 1679, compiling an inventory of the contents of the house. Friends or neighbours perhaps, in sober attire, as befitted the occasion. The figure seated at the table board made use of quill pen and parchment to record, '.... *one paire of andirons .... one spitt .... one dripping pann ....'* Then our thoughts turned to the bread oven, the whereabouts of which we had just been told, and to the mullioned window beyond, unglazed and at that time looking out over Yeoman Bryant Heasey's 'backside' (yard). *'Draughty'*, was how Mr Batley described The Passage, thus recalling the fact that hats were once worn indoors to keep out the cold, as in centuries past, such a house would have been draughtier still, inasmuch as the slatted windows were only shuttered at night and there were shrinkage gaps between the timber framing and the wattle and daub walls reaching up to the thatch. He held out a picture and already another was forming, of the land stretching as far as what is now the airfield, and our thoughts far removed from the 1970s houses and gardens which have become a part of the plot, we began to wonder about those who were there when the only 'aircraft' were the birds and the bees. Boys with lovelocks, playing in the orchard .... and their mother in lace-trimmed gown and coif, picking apples perhaps, late in the year .... Twin brooks then flowed through the village street and on the far side stood a cottage built in Tudor times, wherein Master Goddard, the Tailor, had fashioned the doublet and hose worn by our Great Grandfather, John Smith, as he climbed the stairs in the furthest corner of the room described by Mr Batley. The inventory had shown that the chamber over the hall was not the main bedchamber, as that would have contained the feather bed, whereas this had only what we would call a flock mattress and is thus likely to have been occupied by a youthful 'Old William' and his brothers. What colour were the 'hangings', we wondered, and was there a 'hide', or secret room, behind the well-remembered panelling, wherein, in more troublous times, our Great Grandfather may have sought refuge, if Roundheads had burst in through the screens passage in search of those who were for the King? Having read many a stirring tale of that sort, we could picture him hidden there and the scene below like the well-known painting entitled, "And When Did You Last See Your Father?" But who was he?

We still did not know. We had been looking for the elusive baptismal entry which would tie him to John and Christian, the only other Smiths in the parish at that time and had checked both the transcript and the original register, in case of an oversight, as some entries are written so close together that it is hard to tell one from another, yet had still found nothing. The search therefore had to be widened to include all of the parishes in South Oxfordshire. He could, of course, have come from further afield but, if so, we had had no chance of finding a link and were therefore pinning our hopes on the fact that, if not from Chalgrove, he was from one of the nearby parishes. This wider search yielded only two possibilities – John son of John baptized 4th October 1601 and John son of Hercules baptized 8th May 1604, both in Great Milton, the next parish to Chalgrove. We began holding our breath. Could one of them be John of Chalgrove and, if so, would we ever be able to prove it? ....

As before, all Smith entries were extracted from the Great Milton parish register from outset – and little family trees were compiled. If we were unsure of something, a burial for example, it was listed at the side for future reference. Fortunately, the Vicar had noted down one or two abodes, such as the hamlet of Ascott and the village of Little Milton, perhaps because it was such a widespread parish and there were more Smiths therein than we had so far come across, he was trying to differentiate between them. This made it easier to compile the family trees and pointed us in the direction of Ascott, from whence came our two possible Johns. The siblings of the one who was the son of Hercules were found and we also discovered that these two Johns were cousins, as their fathers were brothers, but other than that, we did not seem to be getting anywhere. We needed something to go on and as it was quite a while since we had read the will of John of Chalgrove and, at that time, we had been concerned only with finding proof of 'Old William's' identity, whereas we were now looking for clues to his own, we thought that it might be worth studying it more closely.

We knew, of course, that he was a Yeoman and had seen that he was referred to as a Freeholder in the College lists of manorial tenants, but these terms meant nothing to us then, other than that he owned the land he farmed. It was only as our research into the history of the village progressed and we read more and more documents and became familiar with 17th century society, that we learnt that those words, and the second in particular, meant that he was a well-respected member of that society. By that time, we had also read the book entitled, '*The Village Labourer*' – J. L. and Barbara Hammond, which refers to the social order in a pre-enclosure village such as Chalgrove and includes a list as follows: 1, The lord (or lords) of the manor. (Some villages were divided into more than one manor and there was therefore more than one lord. Such was the case in Chalgrove); 2, <u>Freeholders</u>; 3, Copyholders; 4, Tenant Farmers; 5, Cottagers; 6, Squatters and 7, F a r m servants living in their employer's house.

We also then came to realise that very few people were buried within the Church, rather than in the churchyard, and that those who were, were the elite. Yet even at this early stage, when rereading the will, we recognised that the words, '*.... to be buried in Christian buriall in the Middle Allie in the Church of Chalgrove Aforesayde neere unto the seat I uselly did sitt....*' were a clue to his status. For surely, had he not thought that he was entitled to be buried therein, he would not have made such a request.

Already having found that we had overlooked something so important, we read on, in the hope that we had missed something more, and indeed we had. Something of the utmost importance. Yet still we did not recognise it as such. As time went on and we read hundreds of wills and other documents and became familiar with the ways of 17th century society, with the relationships and the phraseology, we realised that our many times Great Grandfather could not have helped us more. But not then. Indeed we had foolishly remarked upon the fact that he had named Robert Quatermaine and Roger Symmes as his executors, rather than having chosen

trusted relatives, which we later learnt was almost always the case. These he had referred to as his '*loveing brothers*' and we had therefore assumed that they were such close friends that this was a term of endearment used at that time. But we then gave it some more thought and began to wonder ....
For although we were still fairly new to the reading of wills, we had seen enough to know by then that the term 'brother' always applied either to a brother or a brother-in-law, whereas a friend, no matter how close or dearly-loved, was never usually referred to as anything other than that. So what did that mean?.... Now that time has passed and we have read those aforementioned hundreds of wills and more, from the 16th to the 19th centuries, we know, without a shadow of a doubt, that the word brother referred only to one's true brother, half-brother, step-brother, brother-in-law or to the brother-in-law of a spouse or sibling.

We have also come across something which family historians who are not yet back to the 16th or 17th century may find it useful to know. For during that period, a nephew or niece was usually referred to as a cousin in this part of Oxfordshire, and therefore possibly elsewhere, and only very occasionally was the newer terminology used. This can cause confusion, as cousins were, of course, also called cousins, as were the sons and daughters of a cousin. For there were no first, second or third cousins. One therefore has to allow for the fact that whilst a cousin may actually be a cousin, he or she may, in some instances, be a nephew or niece! Similarly, whilst a son-in-law <u>was</u> a son-in-law, this could also refer to a stepson, although the term brother-in-law was never used, or certainly not in this part of Oxfordshire.

This brings us back to the question of how Robert Quatermaine and Roger Symmes came to be John of Chalgrove's brothers. In the case of Robert Quatermaine, it seemed obvious. John Smith was married to Avis Quatermaine and Robert was therefore surely her brother. Out came the family tree of Daniel and Elizabeth Quatermaine (née Symeon), our 9/10 x Great Grandparents on the distaff side, that we might verify the fact before moving on to Roger Symmes. There before us was Avis (baptized 1610), their eldest daughter, there were her sisters and there were her brothers – Rodolph, Richard, William and Daniel ....! Could we have misread one of the entries? Was the unusual name of Rodolph (Latin for Ralph) really Robert? At the earliest opportunity, we checked the parish register, but there was no doubt whatsoever. Avis did not have a brother by the name of Robert!

The only other possibility as far as we could see, was that he had married John's sister, but when we came to look for the entry, there were none which fitted. We had thus to find out who he was and that meant attempting to sort out a multitude of Quatermaines. For although this is a somewhat unusual name, it was then common in Chalgrove, whereas Smith was not! It was therefore indeed fortunate that the Vicar had tried to differentiate between those with the most common Christian names, by referring to them as *'John the Butcher'*, for example, *'John of the hair lip'*, or *'Francis on the Green'*, etc. As in the search for John Smith of Chinnor (later of Saunderton Lee), index cards were used to help with this mammoth task. The most common Quatermaine Christian names were John, William and Francis and each of those with any of these names were given blue, pink or yellow cards respectively, showing the date of baptism and the parents' names. Thankfully there were far fewer Roberts, but as they were of particular interest, they were given the green cards. Further cards, in the relevant colour, were made out for events, such as marriages, burials and baptisms of children and, still more with the date of each document witnessed by, or containing a reference to, one of them.

We then began reading all Quatermaine wills from the 16th to early 18th century and compiling little family trees from the information contained therein. If certain that someone referred to in a will was one of those for whom we had already made out an index card, the information was added to it. If not, another card was written. Most of the wills were witnessed by other Quatermaines and thus provided us with either a recognisable signature or a distinctive mark, whereby the witness could be identified. This also enabled us to see how many by each name were alive at a particular time. For example, if a John Quatermaine witnessed a will in 1670 and the same signature or mark was found to belong to a testator in 1705, we knew that this John was alive throughout that period and that he was old enough to have been a witness in 1670. If there were two different John Quatermaine signatures/marks on a document dated 1690, this then told us that there were three John Quatermaines alive at that time. It was interesting to see the different styles of writing, those from the earlier times having spelt Francis with a double F, for instance, and formed the letter Q in a more ornate way and an E like the letter O with a line through the middle, whereas the younger generation wrote in a more fashionable way, using only a single F and forming their letters much as we do today. A description of each signature was put on to the relevant coloured card, or the mark was copied thereon, together with the date and details of the document witnessed. Further signatures were obtained from the wills of those with other surnames, into whose families Quatermaines had married, and these were also a source of information, as were the Depositions (1542–1639), transcribed by Jack Howard-Drake. For when giving evidence in the Church Courts, which several Quatermaines did, a person had to give his or her name, age and place of birth and there is often other useful and interesting information included therein, such as the place of residence and how long the deponent had lived there, relationships, if any, and occasionally his or her occupation.

When all of the information was collated, we studied the family trees in conjunction with the index cards and if, for example, there was a Roger Quatermaine with a brother called John and a John Quatermaine had witnessed his will, it then seemed likely that that signature belonged to that particular John Quatermaine. We therefore checked to see if he could still be alive at the relevant date and whether there was any evidence to say that he was. If he had other brothers or close relatives on whose wills that signature was found, it was almost certain that it was him and the index card was marked accordingly. By this means, we gradually began to see who was who and as the little trees had by this time begun to fit together, it soon became clear that all of the Quatermaines who have played an interesting part in the history of Chalgrove, were descended from two families, that of a John Quatermaine who was taxed after he had died! (Lay Subsidy 1523, *'John Quatermayn obiit'* – deceased) and Roger and Alice, whose grandson, Roger (born circa 1534), had seventeen children, twelve of whom were sons. It seems probable that these two lines became one further back, but as the purpose of this part of our research was to discover which of the Robert Quatermaines was the brother of our John Smith, we left it there and turned our attention to the three adult Roberts alive in 1676, when John's will was written. There would have been four, but there is no record whatsoever of the one baptized in 1605, son of John, and it therefore seems likely that he died during the gap in the register and was perhaps slain in the Civil War. That therefore left us with two in Chalgrove and one in nearby Newington, whom I have listed below and have given the letters, **B**, **C** and **D** to make them easier to identify. The Robert labelled **A** has been included although he had died by then, as he has an important part to play....

A ROBERT baptized 1579/80; buried January 1669/70 (son of Roger and Cicely)

B ROBERT baptized 1616; buried January 1680/1 (son of **A**)

C ROBERT baptized 1626; buried 1705 (son of John, the butcher; thought to be nephew of **A**)

D ROBERT of NEWINGTON born circa 1650; died 1697 (son of Richard and Martha; and grandson of **A**)

It was indeed fortunate that John of Chalgrove's brother had signed both his will and his inventory and that he had a neat and easily recognisable signature, for we quickly established, by referring to our research, that he was **B**, the youngest son of Robert **(A)** and Elizabeth. The all-important question was, however, how did he, a Quatermaine, come to be the brother of John Smith? We knew that he was not the brother of Avis Quatermaine, the wife of John Smith, nor had he married John's sister. His own will had confirmed that he had married Anne Greening during the gap in the register and that after she had died in 1668 along with her eight month old daughter, Avis, named after his aforementioned sister-in-law, he had wed Frances Wade, who is referred to on the plaque in the Church. What then was the answer? ....

We studied his family in depth, trying to find a clue, then at last we spotted it. Angela had long since been puzzled by a marriage entry in 1611. 'Who is this Elizabeth Smith?', she had repeatedly asked, for she was not amongst any of the Smith baptisms which we had extracted from the Chalgrove parish register, nor was she on any of the little family trees. But though unable to answer that question, we had never bothered to try to find out. It was of no importance at the time. Now though, it was of the utmost importance. For she had married a Robert Quatermaine!!! Of course, it was not Robert, the brother **(B)**, as he had not yet been born. She had, however, married the only Robert Quatermaine who was of a marriageable age at the time – his father!!! **(A)** This therefore meant that the mother of Robert Quatermaine **(B)**, who was the brother of our John Smith (John of Chalgrove), was Elizabeth <u>Smith</u>!!! Was she then also the mother of John of Chalgrove? For that would indeed have made Robert **(B)** his brother ....

A widow with a child was then well-sought-after. More than one child meant more mouths to feed, but just the one proved that she was not barren, which was important to farming families with property to pass on down. But at this early stage, useful information, such as whether someone was from another parish, or was widowed at the time of marriage, was seldom recorded in the parish register. On the odd occasion, the Vicar would write '*of Milton*', for example, in order to differentiate perhaps, if there was someone in the parish with the same name, but between 1564 and 1637, there were no remarks whatsoever amongst the marriage entries, yet at least five widowers were married during that time. We therefore thought it likely that there were many more omissions, perhaps relating to the women, who were then considered to be of much less importance – at least one woman was buried as '*the wife of....*', without even the benefit of a Christian name. But was one such omission the fact that the Elizabeth Smith who married Robert Quatermaine **(A)** in 1611, was a widow from the nearby parish of Great Milton? As we began studying the manorial records in depth and thus covered the various little gaps in the register, we felt sure that in her case there must have been at least one omission, for as the only Smiths then in Chalgrove were John and Christian and their children, this Elizabeth had to have come from somewhere else. It was therefore indeed hopeful that Robert Quatermaine's **(A)** eldest brother, Ralph, had gone to Great Milton in search of a wife, as did another brother, Luke. But did <u>he</u>? Or did Elizabeth walk by the stream which flows from Ascott Farm past Chalgrove Manor, where he was later found to be living, and was that how they met? How we longed to know. For John of Chalgrove's two possible baptisms in 1601 (son of John) and 1604 (son of Hercules) were both in Great Milton.... in the hamlet of Ascott, which is just along the lane from Chalgrove ....

The possibility of Hercules Smith having been his father was soon ruled out, as he was found to have witnessed a document in 1612 and his wife could not therefore have been a widow marrying in 1611. That left us with John, eldest son of William Smith of Ascott, baptized 1558 and buried 1603 .... (There was, of course, the remote possibility that this burial could have referred to the child, but that seemed unlikely, as the Vicar had been writing *'son of ....'*, *'daughter of ....'*, etc., when recording burials.) But did he marry an Elizabeth?

Whilst pursuing this line of research, we had also been trying to find out about Roger Symmes, the other *'loveing brother'*, and had discovered that he was descended from John Symmes Alias <u>Smith</u> (buried January 1601/2). Alias, meaning 'also known as', seems to have denoted that the parents of the child being baptized were unmarried and thereafter became part of the person's name, as in a double-barrelled surname. The alias sometimes continued for several generations, in one instance for at least 180 years. It was also sometimes used to identify a widow who had remarried. For example, Sibbyll, widow of Edward Saywell, who later married Nicholas Butler, was buried as Sibbyll Saywell Alias Butler, and Joan, widow of Stephen Smith, who later married Thomas Herbert, as Joan Smith Alias Herbert. The children of John Symmes Alias Smith were baptized simply as Symmes, but his granddaughter, Mary, the sister of the aforementioned Roger, was baptized Symmes Alias Smith in 1602, after which the alias was dropped. The coupling of these two names, albeit very early on, looked hopeful and we searched all of the surrounding parishes for some further connection between Roger and our John of Chalgrove, but this came to nothing.

Returning therefore to the search for the marriage of John Smith, son of William of Ascott, this had to have taken place between 1570 – for although unlikely, someone <u>could</u> then marry at the age of twelve years – and 1603 – if he had married after his son, John, was born. The Oxfordshire Marriage Index yielded no possible entries in Great Milton however, and only one in Chalgrove, that of John Smith and Christian Child 18th October 1603, and as the John in question had died in the June of that year, this was ruled out. Of the twenty-three remaining marriages, only four had taken place in nearby parishes: 12th November 1576 at Drayton St Leonard to Yeadie Godfree, 6th October 1577 at Brightwell Baldwin to Anne Winchester, 21st November 1577 at Brightwell Baldwin to Katherine Wise and 10th September 1599 at Drayton St Leonard to Elizabeth Wise.

One of these was also immediately ruled out, as we found a Bond of Administration dated 1582, relating to a burial entry for a John Smith in Brightwell Baldwin in 1578, which named his widow, *'Katherine Wyse alias Smith'*. We were therefore left with three possible marriages, but for either of the earliest two to be right, the couple would have had to have been married for twenty-four or twenty-five years before a child was born, which seemed most unlikely; whereas the third having taken place on 10th September 1599, fitted with the baptism of a son in 1601. Moreover, there were no John Smiths of marriageable age in the parish of Drayton St Leonard at that time, so the groom had to have come from elsewhere. The John for whom we were searching could, of course, have married further afield but, if so, we would probably never know. We had had thus to work on the assumption that the marriage had taken place somewhere in the vicinity of Ascott, and were surprised to see from the map that Drayton St Leonard was actually in close proximity to it. In fact, as our research progressed, we discovered that John Smith, the son of William of Ascott, was then leasing land at Holcombe, which is even nearer to Drayton St Leonard and, when visiting the area, we saw that his land reached almost as far as the village wherein Elizabeth Wise was living, if not further.

This marriage was certainly looking hopeful, but there was still more evidence to collect. It was most important that he had married an Elizabeth, for unless his widow had had that name, there was nothing to tie the 1601 baptism in Great Milton to John of Chalgrove. Our next search was thus for all marriages of a John Smith and an Elizabeth of any surname, during the aforementioned period, and yielded only three possibilities: John Smith and Elizabeth Barfott 29th January 1581, North Leigh; John Smith and Elizabeth Zarcheade 4th April 1583, Oxford St Aldate and John Smith and Elizabeth

Wise 10th September 1599, Drayton St Leonard. Again two of these were rather early, when taking into account the fact that the child was born in 1601.

We now turned our attention to the Elizabeth Smith who had married Robert Quatermaine **(A)** in 1611 and began by searching for the marriage of an Elizabeth of any surname, to someone by the name of Smith, between 1582–1611, in any parish. The earliest date was decided upon, as she had to have been of child-bearing age in 1616, when her last child, Robert Quatermaine **(B)**, was born, and was therefore unlikely to have been more than forty-six years of age at that time, which suggests a date of birth in 1570 or later. To this we added twelve years, to arrive at a starting date for her first marriage, as we had to allow for the fact that, although unlikely, it was then permissible to marry at the early age of twelve years. The later date was, of course, the year in which an Elizabeth Smith married Robert Quatermaine **(A)**. This search resulted in eleven potential marriages, only one of which was anywhere near Chalgrove, where the marriage to Robert Quatermaine took place, that of John Smith and Elizabeth Wise on 10th September 1599, at Drayton St Leonard ....

We had long since ruled out the possibility of the Elizabeth Smith who had married Robert Quatermaine **(A)** having been the <u>sister</u> of John of Chalgrove, as once we acquired more Quatermaine signatures and were thus able to determine which of the Roberts was his brother, we could see that that would have made Robert Quatermaine **(A)** his brother, instead of Robert Quatermaine **(B)**.

Illegitimacy was considered, but the only possible John Smith – the son of Nicholas Smith Junior of Ascott and Elizabeth Mose – was baptized 26th February 1611/12 in Chalgrove and buried a week later. (The mother then had another illegitimate child by a different man and died single within a few years.)

In case John of Chalgrove was related to Robert Quatermaine **(B)** through Robert's wife, Anne Greening, the Greening family were studied in depth, as Anne's grandmother was Anne <u>Smith</u> by her second marriage, but no relationship was found.

Now we had only to check on who Robert Quatermaine **(A)** <u>could</u> have married. In order to do this, we searched for the baptisms, marriages and burials of all Elizabeth Smiths (1570–1611) and, (other than those who were nowhere near there), there were only two in Great Haseley, one in Benson and the Elizabeth Wise who was thought to have become Elizabeth Smith of Ascott. None of the first three would have brought about any sort of relationship between John of Chalgrove and either Robert Quatermaine **(B)** or Roger Symmes, whereas if it was the last Elizabeth who had married Robert Quatermaine **(A)**, her son – John Smith – would have become the brother of both of them ....

As time went on, further evidence came to light which proved that the marriage of John Smith and Elizabeth Wise on 10th September 1599, at Drayton St Leonard, was the right one. But as yet, we did not know that John Smith, the son of William of Ascott, was leasing land at Holcombe, which was next to Drayton St Leonard, or that Elizabeth's brother was named as a *'well-beloved friend'* in one of the Ascott wills – <u>the</u> most relevant one. In fact, we did not even know that there <u>were</u> any Ascott wills ....

The eldest daughter of a wealthy farming family of Drayton St Leonard, Elizabeth was baptized on 17th November 1575 and was thus aged nearly thirty-six when her marriage to Robert Quatermaine **(A)** took place, yet bore him five children in five years. Her ten-year-old son, John Smith, (later of Chalgrove) was therefore soon blessed with a sister Cicely Quatermaine (baptized 26th July 1612) and brothers, Richard Quatermaine (baptized 10th April 1614) and Robert Quatermaine **(B)** (baptized 1st May 1616). Sadly, twin daughters, Dorothye and Jone, were baptized and buried in 1615. (It is interesting to note that twins occur at least once in almost every generation of Quatermaines in Chalgrove and therefore probably account for their name, Quatre, meaning four, and main, meaning hand, and for their coat-of-arms, which resembles four hands raised as if in defence of the monarch).

Just as John of Chalgrove had said in his will, Robert Quatermaine **(B)** was indeed his brother, as Elizabeth Quatermaine (formerly Smith, née Wise) was the mother of both of them, and so indeed was Roger Symmes. For <u>his</u> elder brother, John Symmes, had married Cicely Quatermaine, the daughter of Robert Quatermaine **(A)** and Elizabeth Quatermaine (formerly Smith, née Wise), which meant that in Canon Law Roger became Cicely's brother and therefore the brother of her brother, John Smith! (John of Chalgrove) By the time that John of Chalgrove made his will in 1676, both John Symmes and Richard Quatermaine (the son of Robert Quatermaine **(A)** and Elizabeth, as above) had died, which meant that Robert Quatermaine **(B)** and Roger Symmes were his only surviving brothers.

It all fitted together perfectly, but with a name like Smith one has to have something concrete – something which will leave not a shadow of a doubt – which was why we continued to dig deeper. Wills had helped us this far and were therefore our first thought, but as there were none for those at Ascott, we were somewhat at a loss to know where to look next. One of the files fell open at a long-ago list of Smith wills and, rather than do nothing, we decided to request the few remaining from places which, though nearby, were not thought to be connected, which was how we came to be reading that of John Smythe, Husbandman of Berwyke, (Berrick Salome – once part of the parish of Chalgrove), dated 1534. The handwriting of such an early will, was far from easy to decipher, but at least it was in English, rather than in Latin and I was ready to jot down anything which might be of use. Not that we thought that there would be anything. Angela was saying, '.... *To Alice, daughter of John Smyth .... of ....*' and one could have heard a pin drop. She was poring over the next word and it came at last like a bolt from the blue! '.... *Askott!*'

John of Ascott!' we both exclaimed. For it seemed to be referring to our earliest ancestor, from whom we felt sure that John of Chalgrove was descended. Angela read on, as avidly as the handwriting would allow, every word now suddenly all-important. For William and Nicholas Smith of Ascott, whose burials, amongst other entries, had been extracted from the Great Milton parish register, were thought to be the youngest sons of the aforementioned John of Ascott, and the said William was the father of John of Chalgrove's father, John of Holcombe (baptized 1558 and buried 1603), who had married Elizabeth Wise, later Quatermaine. Such an early document containing such vital information was more than we could ever have hoped for. For as Angela pointed out, a man had had no need to make a will at that time, as the law was such that the property would have automatically passed to his eldest son. We therefore owe our good fortune to the fact that John Smythe of Berwyke (to whom we have since given the name 'Tudor John', as he lived during the reigns of Henry VII and Henry VIII) had had <u>two</u> sons ....

Of the many bequests set down in the will, this chapter is concerned only with one, the part of the property to which we are now about to come. Hungry for information, we were hanging on every word and there was indeed a surprise in store for us. I am not sure what we may have been hoping for, but whatever it was, those words describing the gift of a father to his son in centuries past, by far surpassed anything which we could ever have dreamed of.

> '.... *Item my wylle ys that John my sonn shale have hold and enioy to hym and to hys herys for evermor one tenement in bensyngton with ix acreys of lande and medow to the same tenement pertenynge and belongynge. Item I be queyth to the same John one mesuage and ix acres of lande lyinge and beynge in the fyelds of bensyngton berwyke Roke and Ewelme to hyme and hys heres for evermor.'*

We had had no need to ask ourselves where we had seen these two properties before. For we knew at once – in the will of George Smith, second son of John of Chalgrove! He must have received them as part of a marriage settlement, as they were not in his father's will, yet neither was the monetary settlement bestowed upon younger brother, Daniel, which is referred to in his inventory. The eldest son, John, who inherited the freehold property in Chalgrove and the youngest, Robert, did not marry until after their father had died, but, as previously mentioned, George, Daniel and William would certainly have received settlements, to provide for their widows if that became necessary: George the properties in *'bensyngton berwyke Roke and Ewelme'*, (both cottages were in the hamlet of Roke, which straddled the fragmented boundaries of these parishes, which is why they were all referred to) which would have been considered secondary to that in Chalgrove, and the younger ones monetary amounts. Evidence in support of this, was later found amongst the Lincoln College manorial records, in a document relating to the first Court Baron held after the date of George's marriage, which reads, *'John Smith heath alinated his lands untoe his soon Georg Smith and wee find a relife due unto the lords of this maner which is 4d'*. This is another example of the fact that only *'his lands'* were referred to. The 4d relief was, however, the nominal rent for the Lincoln College cottage and thereafter, George was shown in the list of Lincoln College Freeholders alongside his father, and that he had received that cottage is clearly documented. As to the cottage held from Magdalen College, it was not until John of Chalgrove died that George appeared in the list of Free Tenants. Whether that was because part of the marriage settlement was received at the time of the marriage, in order to provide the couple with an income, and the part which was to provide for the widow, later, or whether it was because the occupants were relatives (Avis Smith's sister having married someone by the name of Prickett) and John of Chalgrove therefore preferred to maintain the cottage himself, rather than trust his son to do so, we can only surmise. Returning, however, to George's will, he bequeathed both properties to his eldest son, George, (1671–1724) and they were subsequently sold to the occupants, who then appear in the tenant lists in his stead, perhaps as he found the upkeep troublesome, inasmuch as he was living some distance away, in Wolvercote. (George Senior had married Ursula, daughter of Richard Hall, yeoman of Wolvercote, in 1670, later headed the list of inhabitants in that parish, and was found in the Quarter Sessions as a Juryman for Wootton Hundred in 1691 and 1703. The younger George and his descendants had a flat stone in the middle aisle of Wolvercote Church, near the chancel arch.)

How had the properties passed from 'Tudor John' to John of Chalgrove though? Here was the proof for which we had been searching – the link between him and the earlier Smiths of Ascott – but a part of that link was missing and we were puzzled ....

For although both William and Nicholas Smith of Ascott held freehold land and were usually at the head of the list of manorial tenants in Roke and Berrick, neither of them had left a will. In fact, there was nothing whatsoever relating to Ascott, not even an inventory. Admittedly, many such documents have not survived, but nevertheless, it did seem a bit strange. Could we have missed something? We looked again, then wished that we hadn't! For we had come across a bond in 1637, granting administration to Elizabeth, widow of John Smith – and the place? Ascott! It seemed like the end of everything. For if it was 'our' Elizabeth, she could not have married Robert Quatermaine (A). Nor could the baptism of her son, in 1601, be that of John of Chalgrove, as the burial entry Anno Domini 1603 June *'the 9th daye John Smithe of Ascott buryed'* could not have related to her husband if he did not die until 1637, and would thus have had to have been that of her son, the 1601 John Smith.

We had felt so sure that he was our John that, in the absence of any further documents, we hardly knew what to do to either prove this or try to disprove it. Through a blur of disconsolation, I saw that Angela had reached for the Oxfordshire probate records index (1516–1732), as she so often had, but expected nothing. Then all at once she was snatching up another of the three volumes and there was suddenly a glimmer of hope! For she had come across a map in the notes at the front of one book which had referred her to the other, as although we had assumed that this map gave the location of parishes, it was, in fact, showing details of 'Peculiars' and Great Milton was one of them! To explain, whereas the majority of parishes in Oxfordshire came under the jurisdiction of the Bishop and Archdeacon of Oxford for the purpose of proving a will, a 'Peculiar' came under separate jurisdiction, such as the Dean and Chapter of Lincoln, in the case of Great Milton. All of the 'Peculiar' wills etc., whatever the date, are listed in the third volume of the probate records index, even though this generally covers the period 1733–1857. Hence our assumption that there were no wills relating to Ascott. Once aware of this oversight, we found what we were looking for – a will for William Smith in 1605, a will and inventory for Nicholas Smith in 1608 and 1612, and an inventory for John Smith in 1603. It was this last upon which we were pinning our hopes, inasmuch as had the burial to which it belonged, been that of a child (the 1601 John), there would not have been an inventory – and there was something more .... Although rather than raise false hopes which could so easily be dashed, Angela was keeping this to herself – the reference for the Bond of Administration was not listed under the 'Peculiars'. Indeed it was not even in the same book as the other Ascott wills etc. ....

The circumstances were such, that the days leading up to our proposed visit to the Oxfordshire Record Office passed slowly. It was a spur-of-the-moment visit, fitted in on a day which we had arranged to spend at Magdalen College Archives. Thus pressed for time, we had meant to arrive at the moment the doors opened, but that was the first thing which went wrong and things continued in the same vein.

The Bond of Administration, dated 1637, was brought to us and it at once became evident that it had been in water. All that could be deciphered was *'Elizabeth Smith the relict and adminx of all and singular the goods, chattells and credits of John Smith late of Astcott'*! Although we did manage to ascertain that the inventory therewith was *'taken at the time of his death'* and appraised on 24th March 1636. The agony was therefore prolonged. Awaiting us at the desk, were the other documents, but there was a shadow hanging over us and unless it was somehow lifted, we could not bring ourselves to look upon what might have been. Angela thought quickly and rushed over to the shelves. Back with a transcript of a parish register, she turned the pages in great haste and finally found what she was looking for, and oh, what a relief! There was the burial to which the Bond of Administration referred – in Ascott-under-Wychwood! Thankfully she had remembered seeing the place in the list of wills and, hardly daring to hope that that was why the reference was in a different book to the other Ascott wills, had reached for the parish register. What we had suffered because of the omission of one word and one letter *'under W.'* from the wills list! (We later checked the wills list again and found that this John's widow did have *'under W.'* beside her name in 1641; and the same error had occurred in respect of Roger Poole and his widow in the same parish.) It was over though and there was just time to glance at the will of William Smith. For no more than a glance was required, inasmuch as such a small fragment of it remained, that apart from some goods left to son, Hercules, and his children, it was of no use.

Our fortunes had now begun to improve though and continued to do so, in that more references to Nicholas Smith and to John of Chalgrove were found amongst the manorial records held by Magdalen College. During the 17th century, even a Freeholder had had to put in an appearance at the Manor Court and at the early age of sixteen years, John was fined for not having done so. It was so nice to see him there, just starting out in life, the more so as he had so nearly lost his identity, and warmed by the thought of a tall, Cavalierly figure in bucket-top boots and broad-brimmed hat, stood amongst those meeting at the cross, at Chalgrove, we returned to the Oxfordshire Record Office at the end of that lovely, sunny afternoon. There was so little time before the doors were to close, that rather than waste a single second putting belongings into a locker, I remained in the car, whilst Angela hurried inside. Few though those minutes of waiting were, I have seldom known any which were longer. At last though, she reappeared and came flying across the car park, her face one enormous smile.

'Nicholas has done it! Nicholas has done it!' she cried and, still gasping for breath, managed to share with me the delights found within. She had looked first at the inventory of John Smith of Ascott, 1603, and had learnt that the burial in June 1603, was indeed that of the son of William Smith (1558–1603) and the father of the 1601 John Smith. A sheep farmer leasing land at Holcombe (hence the fact that he is known to us as John of Holcombe, to differentiate from the other John Smiths) he died at the height of the sheep shearing season, which leads us to wonder whether some sort of accident whilst performing the task, resulted in blood poisoning. For in an age before the discovery of antiseptic and antibiotics, a cut could be lethal. The inventory lists his 200 sheep, the most that we had theretofore come across, beasts (cows), horses, crops and only a few pieces of furniture (as he was perhaps still living at Ascott). Nicholas Smith Senior is mentioned, as having taken away the crops in the *'pasture and meadow ground'* and for retaining money owing to John of Holcombe for wool.

The clock at the Record Office was moving on and there was only just time to reach for the final document, the will of the said Nicholas Smith, yeoman of Ascott. Very advanced in years when he set about making the will, he was the son and heir of John of Ascott, who was the eldest son of 'Tudor John' and was named in the will of 1534. Nicholas was a kindly old gentleman and seems to have been very close to his late brother William's eldest son, the aforementioned John of Holcombe, to his wife and child and to her brother, John Wise, his *'wellbeloved'* friend, whom he chose to be the overseer of his will. The will affords the impression that Elizabeth is taking care of him and that he looked upon her small son, John, (later of Chalgrove), as <u>his</u> grandson, rather than his brother's grandson, as he had no grandchildren of his own. This was perhaps why he bequeathed some of his property to him. For William, having been forced to sell his land shortly before he died, had had nothing to leave to his sons and grandsons. In Nicholas' own words, Bless him,

> *'.... I give and bequeath unto John Smith my daughter in lawes* [referred to as Elizabeth Smith elsewhere in the will] *sone all the Right and interest wch I have at the day of the date hereof of in and to my freeland and tenements in Roke Berwicke and Bensington wth all and singuler their appurtenances To have and to hold to him the said John Smith his heires and Assignes for ever ....'*

He had given us the link which we needed to prove the line back to 1534 and the word 'elated' cannot even begin to describe how we felt! Since then we have thought of him as one of our 'Grandfathers' and he has become as dear to us as they are. His kindness to that fatherless child and to his widowed mother, Elizabeth, who had become, as he says, <u>his</u> daughter-in-law, has bridged the centuries and left no doubt that 'Tudor John', the Husbandman of Berwyke, was our twelve-times and thirteen-times Great Grandfather!

Signature of John Smith, yeoman and freeholder of Chalgrove (1601–79) from the will of William Quatermaine, proved 1640. Reproduced by kind permission of Oxfordshire History Centre.

14th of Aprill Anno Dono 1679 prized by us
whose names are here under written

Imprimis his money purse and apparrell   2-0-0

It in the Halle on table on Cubbord
with other Lumber   1-1-4

It in the Halle Chimney on paire of Andirons
two hangers fire shauell tongs on spitt
on front dripping pann prized at   0-6-0

It in the parlor on table on carpitt
three Joyned stooles two chaires on litle
side table three Cushings two Joyn...
in the Chimney prized at   1-8-6

It in the milke house on Iron ... on safe
on chees presse on powdering trough
with other Lumber prized at   0-8-8

It in the pump roome Brasse and pewter
prized at   1-11-7

It in the Buttery fower barrell one
kneading trough and other Lumber
prized at   0-10-3

It in ... in on Iron Bound five
paires of Bacon and other Lumber
prized at   2-15-9

It in the Chamber ouer the Halle
on flock bed on bedstead and hangings
on Couerlet on blankett and other
Lumber prized at   0-19-10

It in the Chamber ouer the parlor
one bedstead one feather bed two
Coueled and other Lumber
Couerlett and blankett prized at   1-12-8

It in the Chamber ouer the Buttery
on old bed and bedstead two blanketts
and other Lumber prized at   0-1-8

It in the Chamber ouer the parlor
twelue paire of sheets six pillow
cases two table clothes two dozen
of Napkins prized at   3-18-3

Part of the inventory of John Smith, yeoman and freeholder of Chalgrove, taken on the day that he died, 14th April 1679. Reproduced by kind permission of Oxfordshire History Centre.

*The Quatremaine Memorial on the west wall of St Mary's Church, Chalgrove. The Elizabeth Quatremaine named thereon was the mother of John Smith of Chalgrove and the Robert Quatremaines named are **A, B** and **D** respectively.*

Ford Cottage, Drayton St Leonard.

9

Tudor Tapestry

Is it possible to trace one's family history beyond the start of the parish registers? The question had been put to Dr Robin Darwall-Smith, archivist at Magdalen College, Oxford, and the answer was accompanied by a regretful shake of the head. For before that there is no proof of who was who. Indeed there were few surnames, as such, prior to the 15th century. Yet how could we complain? We had never expected to find Grandad Smith, let alone reach back another four centuries into Tudor times and, even then, it was our good fortune to edge just that little bit further than the very first entries in the parish register. Of course, we owe that good fortune entirely to our twelve-times and thirteen-times Great Grandfather, John Smythe, Husbandman of Berwyke, whom we refer to as 'Tudor John', in order to differentiate from all of the other John Smiths in our family. For it was only because he made a will – one of the earliest to survive – at a time when there was no need to do so, that we were able to forge the link. Without that, we would never have found any of our ancestors prior to John of Chalgrove and would have had no proof as to who he was. Yet it was such a tenuous thread whereby so much depended, inasmuch as if only one of 'Tudor John's' sons had outlived him, the will may never have been made. For in 1534, when it was proved, the property passed to the eldest son by common law. Thus if there was only the one, or this complied with a man's wishes, he had had no need to set them down. 'Tudor John' was, however, a fair-minded man and was determined that his sons should share and share alike. This is evident throughout the will. For John, the elder of the two, received the *'best coffer'* and Richard the second best, Richard the *'best iron cart'* and John the *'second best cart shooed with iron'*. He then received the *'best brass pott'* and Richard the *'second brass pott'* and the will continued in this vein until all of the goods were disposed of, and, that Richard might be as well provided for as his brother, more property was purchased just prior to the drafting of the document and the purchase referred to therein.

It was in the Forge at Chalgrove, a Magdalen College copyhold property, that Richard started out however, and this he held from 1520 until at least 1551. (Magdalen Rentals and Survey). But as there is evidence to show that he was living in nearby Brightwell Baldwin by 1545, he must have passed the Forge to one of his sons, shortly after inheriting the two freehold properties from his father, and it remained in Smith hands until the late 16th century. Whilst the lease continued to be in Richard's name, he would have been listed in the Rentals and Survey, whether or not he was living there, as only the owners were recorded in these documents. This is evident from the fact that some tenants held as many as three properties, all of which included a dwelling house, and can only have been living in one of them, yet are listed against all three.

Having extracted all of the Smith entries from the parish registers pertaining to Chalgrove (including Berrick Salome), Brightwell Baldwin, Great Milton, Stadhampton, Warborough and all of the surrounding parishes, as well as some further afield, read all of the Smith wills and a great many others which were thought to perhaps be of use, and studied the manorial records throughout that early period, we knew who was where and when they were there. The manorial records had also shown that neither of the freehold properties bequeathed to Richard, were in Chalgrove, Roke or Berrick Salome, which fitted with the fact that there were only three Richard Smiths thereabouts during the mid-to-late 16th century – all in the adjoining parish of Brightwell Baldwin. The proof that one of them was ours, was contained in the will (proved 1545) of Elizabeth Wackelyn (Walkelen) of that parish, the widow of the overseer of his father's will. For *'John Smyth of Hascot'*, was the overseer and witness of the 1545 document, and Richard a beneficiary and as these two sons of 'Tudor John' were the overseers of her late husband's will in 1534, the chances of the Richard in her will being anyone other than John of Ascott's brother, are less than negligible. Moreover, Richard and Isobel (a derivative of Elizabeth) Smith are named together and the parish register shows that it was *'Richard Smyth of the Pond'* (explanation to follow) who was married to Elizabeth (burial entry 15th August 1568, *'Elizabeth Smith wife of Richard of the Pond'*) whereas the only other two Richard Smiths were married to Agnes (will of *'Richard Smyth of Bradyeates'* and Lay Subsidies) and Margaret (will of *'Richard Smyth the Younger of Overtowne'*). Our Richard was amongst the beneficiaries who were simply named in the will of Elizabeth Wackelyn, which denoted that they were from Brightwell Baldwin, as those who were from other parishes were so described.

This fitted with the fact that his father had left him *'.... the tenement and gardeyne callyd Jacobbs ....'* For as there were no house names, as such, at that time, nor were there any street names and the houses were not numbered, it seems to have been customary to refer to a house by the name of the man who built it, such as Drewes, Kents, Olivers, Sawyers and Waklands. The first of these, when bequeathed to its subsequent occupier, was referred to as a *'cotage called Dryws house'* and he was thereafter known as Thomas Spyre of Drewes. Proof that our theory is correct was found in the early manorial records, as there are entries in the Magdalen College Rentals and Court

Books as follows: 1520 John Quatermaine *'for a messuage and yard land* [virgate] *late Richard Saunders'* with a note added that this later passed to his widow Elizabeth; and 1558 Elizabeth Quatermaine received a *'messuage and virgate called Saunders'*. Similarly, the next entry in the Rental told us that the same John Quatermaine held a tenement and half a virgate called Dodds and later entries in the Court Books perpetuated that name when referring to this property, and although we had never come across this surname amongst the records, a John Dodd was then found in a Court Roll from 1462.

The property inherited by Richard, may thus have been built by John Jacob, who was then an inhabitant of Brightwell Baldwin, or his forebears, as we cannot recall having come across the name elsewhere, other than perhaps fleetingly.

As we shall show, 'Tudor John' is thought to have come from Brightwell Baldwin, and the fact that his son was to *'have the tenement and gardeyne callyd Jacobbs accordyng to the graunt made to hym and hys heres by me and Agnes my wyffe ....'* suggests that he may have acquired it by way of marriage, as that would account for Agnes having had some say in to whom it was bequeathed.

The means by which we discovered which of the three Richard Smiths in Brightwell Baldwin was ours, was the will of 'Richard the Younger' of Overtowne (proved 1568), as it was witnessed by *'Richard Smyth of the Pond'* and *'Richard Smyth my older brother'*. For until then we had not known for certain that Robert and Agnes, whose wills we had previously read, had had two sons by that name, or which of the Richards they were. This may seem odd, but because of the high mortality rate during the 16th and early 17th century, it was commonplace to name more than one son after someone special, such as his father, grandfather, godfather, or some illustrious ancestor. Often only one survived, but not always, as in the aforementioned case, which can, of course, complicate matters for the family historian. For example, one branch of Quatermaines had three Johns born consecutively and it is only certain that one died as a child. A Quatermaine in Garsington referred to his brother, Thomas the Elder and his brother, Thomas the Younger and these are further instances which we have come across – Elizabeth Wise, who married John Smith of Holcombe, had two brothers named John, both of whom lived; in his will dated 1617, Reynold Wildgoose names his eldest son, John, son, John the Younger and sons, Thomas the Elder and Thomas the Younger. He obviously had a reason for naming them thus, as there were three other sons, simply called Roger, William and Edward. In the will of Agnes Bedford, widow of Clifton Hampden, dated 1557, she refers to her *'eldest sonne John Bedford'*, *'sonne John Bedford dwelling at Thame'* and *'youngest sonne John Bedford'*! On reading this, we could quite understand why the second son left Clifton Hampden and went to live elsewhere!

These examples illustrate the fact that it was not unusual for brothers to have the same name and in the case of Richard Smith of Bradyeates and Richard Smith the Younger, the sons of Robert and Agnes of Brightwell Baldwin, it was to prove very useful indeed. For the will of one of them was witnessed by the other two Richard Smiths in the village, and as it was clear which were the brothers, we knew that our Richard was *'of the Pond'*, or *'of Ponds'*, as it was sometimes known. But where were the Ponds? A telephone call to a local historian pointed us in the right direction and, with the old Ordnance Survey map as our guide, we set off in search of the three ponds once in Brightwell Park. The site of the one nearest to the village was still discernible and there was only one house (now two cottages) close by. It appeared to have once been a three-bay, single-storey building with an attic, which was thought to have been built in 1652. This is an assumption based on the fact that there is a date carved into a beam in front of the chimney stack, but it could be that that was when the chimney was put in, as is sometimes the case, and the building may be of an earlier period. For whilst researching the houses in Chalgrove, in the hope of discovering where our family were living, we came across one which, we are told, has 1680 carved into the beam over the hearth and that must be when the chimney was constructed, as it does not appear in the Hearth Tax Returns of 1662–6, yet the history of the house, recorded in the manorial records, dates back to at least 1591. The old, timber-framed building by the pond in Brightwell Baldwin, may therefore be older than is thought, but if it does date from 1652, it must have been built on the site of 'the tenement and gardeyne callyd Jacobbs' and would then be the work of Richard's great grandson (another John Smith!), the occupant from 1643–1681.

This part of the village was formerly known as Nethertown, a long-forgotten term used as a suffix in the earliest parish register in order to differentiate between two men with the same name, one of whom lived in Overtowne/Uppertown and the other in the lower part of the village near the church. Further evidence in support of Richard's property having been situated there, was gleaned from wills and inventories, and, by referring to the Hearth Tax of 1662, which was compiled in the order that the parish constables walked, we were able to establish where his descendants were living at that time, and we know from the wills that the house was passed down through the family.

It was indeed fortunate that our Smiths seem to have been the only ones in and around those villages and hamlets in that part of Oxfordshire, who were Freeholders during the 16th-17th century, as this proved most helpful. Certainly in the 16th century, as most people held copyhold houses and/or land from the lord of the manor, if anything occurred in respect of a Freeholder, the fact was noted and even as time went on, the Freeholders were listed separately in the lists of manorial tenants. This therefore helped us to pinpoint who was who.

Copyhold property was passed down through families by

securing a lease of lives, which had to be renewed before the last life (usually the third) ended. Failure to do so, meant that the lord could reclaim the property and raise the rent before re-granting it to whomsoever he chose. Hence the remark sometimes encountered within the pages of the Magdalen College manorial court books, *'.... hangs on one life'*. Each time a new lease was secured, a fine was imposed, thus in order to extend the term for the maximum number of years, the copyholder would often choose a baby or young child as the third life, but if this was a daughter, or a nephew or niece, as soon as a son was born, the property was surrendered to the lord of the manor and re-granted at the Manor Court under a new lease. The high mortality rate led to these leases being renewed fairly frequently in order to ensure that the property was not lost, and the entries in the court books are useful in that they state relationships. The death of a copyholder is also recorded and the widow or next life (holder) is usually named.

The Smith land was held freely however and, by the 16th century, they were therefore under no obligation to render a service to the lord, other than that they were required to pay a nominal rent and attend the Manor Court or send someone with an excuse (essoin). Richard's land passed to his eldest son, John, to whom probate was granted 12th January 1593/4. This is shown by the Lay Subsidy lists and their burial entries, as well as by the fact that later generations were still known as *'of the Pond'/'of Ponds'* until at least the 1760s.

The Lay Subsidy was a tax imposed on land and goods from the 12th to the 17th century and individuals were named in the returns from the early 16th century (and in 1327 and 1332). By comparing these lists of taxpayers with the baptisms and burials in the parish register and taking into account the amount upon which tax was payable, one can often determine relationships. For example, Agnes, widow of Robert Smith (buried 1542) of Brightwell Baldwin, appears in the list in 1542 with goods worth £3 and following her death in 1568, their eldest son, Richard Smith of Bradyeates/The Stone (buried 1577), is shown in 1568, paying for goods worth £3. His widow, Agnes, is then listed in 1577 and the amount is again £3. After her death, the goods and chattels were probably divided between their six children, each of whom would therefore have been below the tax threshold. It is useful to know that a man or his widow were only listed in the place where he or she had the most assets and were taxed on either land or goods, whichever would yield the highest return. Those in our family, having been Freeholders, were easy to locate and follow in the lists inasmuch as they were paying tax on land, whereas all of the other Smiths in Brightwell Baldwin at that time, were paying for goods. In the 1568 Lay Subsidy, our Richard Smith was taxed on land which provided an annual income of twenty-six shillings and eight pence, but must have sold some of the land, or given it to one of his children by 1577, as the amount had then decreased to twenty shillings. The new owner would not have appeared in the list as six shillings and eight pence was below the tax threshold. Richard is again shown in 1581 and the amount upon which tax was payable for his land was still twenty shillings. It continued at this level, although his son, John, became the taxpayer in 1594, which corresponds with the burial entry in the parish register in 1593/4 – *'The VIIth day of January Richard Smith the freeholder was buried'*. (We already knew that this was our Richard's burial, as those of Richard Smyth the Younger and his brother, Richard Smyth of Bradyeates, match the dates of their wills.) The 1599 Lay Subsidy also lists John Smith and twenty shillings. *'John Smith of Overtowne, Freeholder'* was then buried 10th June 1611, and his inventory told us that he had two houses, presumably the one by the pond in Nethertown and one in Uppertown. This suggests that, at some time during Richard's long life, his son was either given land in Uppertown to build upon, or this was the other property which his father inherited from his father, 'Tudor John'.

Both of the aforementioned properties were bequeathed to John's (buried 1611) only surviving son, Anthony, who left the one by the pond to his eldest son, the John Smith who may have rebuilt or extended it in 1652, and the one in Uppertown to his second son, Anthony.

Just to fill in a few gaps, nothing was known of Richard's wife or of his offspring, other than that his eldest son, John, (buried 1611) named in his grandfather's will, was born by 1534. This John's descendants were easy to trace however, as there were only three families of Smiths in Brightwell Baldwin during the 16th century and the vicar having been very thorough, we were able to draw up family trees relating to each of them: 'of Ponds' (ours); 'of Davis' (coming from a John Smith who was buried in 1557 and is thought to have perhaps been the nephew of 'Tudor John'); and those who were descended from Robert and Agnes Smith, formerly of Watlington.

Once we knew that our family were 'of Ponds', the burial of Richard's wife was evident – 15th August 1568, Elizabeth Smith wife of Richard of the Pond. It is interesting to note, that she is referred to as 'Isobel Smyth', in the will of Elizabeth Walkelen, who is herself referred to as 'Esobell' in her husband's will, and Elizabeth Smith, the daughter of Robert and Agnes, is called 'Isobel' in her father's will, this having been a derivative of Elizabeth. (A Magdalen College tenant list dated 1520 shows one woman as Isabel/Elizabeth). Similarly, Jane and Joan were interchangeable, as were Maud and Matilda, and Agnes, Annis and Ann(e).

References to relatives in wills, suggest that Ellen Smith, who married Anthony Edge and Marion, the wife of Rafe Spyer of Brightwell Baldwin, were Richard's daughters, but the lines stemming from these cannot be included in the family tree, as there is, as yet, no real proof. Richard's known descendants remained in Brightwell Baldwin at least until the early 19th century, some having married those whom we encountered whilst studying the manorial records relating to Chalgrove. It was also evident from the wills and inventories that they were in touch with our side of the family, to which we now turn.

Richard's elder brother, John Smith of Ascott, was born long before the start of the parish registers, thus our only clue to his age was the fact that he appears in the Lay Subsidy list of 1517. For having had to have had enough goods and/or land to become a taxpayer, he cannot have been a mere boy at that time, hence the estimated date of birth about 1490 or earlier. He was probably married by 1517, as in less than thirty years, his eldest son was one of the only other two people with enough goods to appear in the Lay Subsidy list for Ascott, a hamlet just over a mile west of Chalgrove and about two and a half miles north of Berwyke (Berrick Salome). The Lay Subsidy returns of 1523, show that John of Ascott was then paying six shillings in tax, (which was six times the amount paid by half of the men listed and more than twice that of the next highest), whilst in nearby Berwyke, his father was at the head of the list, paying forty shillings. He is next named, along with his two eldest children, Alice and John, in the will of his father, which was proved in 1534. The fact that Alice precedes her brother at a time when women were considered of much less importance, shows that she was the eldest grandchild and, as such, she received a monetary bequest. Her younger brother and his cousin, John, son of Richard, were the only other grandchildren named, although the phrase *every on of my chyldrens chyldren* shows that 'Tudor John' had daughters and that there were other grandchildren, belonging to his sons and to their sisters.

Later that year, John of Ascott and his brother, Richard, were named as the executors of the will of (their uncle?) John Walkelen (sometimes spelt Wakelyne) of Brightwell Baldwin, the supervisor/overseer of their father's will, and Ascott Chapel and Berwyke Church received monetary bequests therein. He was then chosen as the overseer of the will of the widow Walkelen in 1545 and was also a witness thereof. The will of John Quatermaine of Berwyke, was witnessed by a *'John Smythe, Forman'*, in 1545 and this is thought to have been John of Ascott, which means that he was then what we would call the spokesman at the Manor Court of Berwyke, Roke and Bensington. Clearly he had become a substantial inhabitant, as had his father in Berwyke, for in the Lay Subsidy of 1546 and 1547, he is at the head of the list in Ascott, paying twenty-six shillings and eight pence for £20 in goods (1546) and sixteen shillings for £16 in goods (1547). The tax threshold had perhaps been raised, as only three men were eligible for taxation, the others having been John Reade and John of Ascott's eldest son, John, both of whom were paying three shillings and four pence for £5 in goods. At that time, this amount of money was worth so much more of course. This is evident from the fact that, in the same year, someone purchased two messuages, a garden, the right to graze three cows and thirty-two acres of land for £30. Just how much this equates to, is apparent when one considers the cost of houses today. The transaction referred to, is recorded in the Feet of Fines, dated 1547, and concerns our John of Ascott and his wife, Elizabeth, on the one part and John Rolles, (prominent in earlier deeds relating to 'Tudor John' and the Walkelyns) who is thought to have been a relative, perhaps his brother-in-law, on the other. The Feet of Fines, held by The National Archives, comprise details of cases heard in the Court of Common Pleas in order to create a record of title to property. These were fictitious legal proceedings, entered into solely for that purpose, and a summary was written in the same words on the left, the right and at the foot of the page, which was then cut apart along wavy lines to prevent forgery. One copy was given to the purchaser, in this case John Rolles, another to the vendor(s), John of Ascott and his wife, and the third was enrolled in the Court of Common Pleas.

The aforementioned property seems to have been a single holding, as we learnt from the manorial records that each individual holding was listed separately, irrespective of the length of its description. For example,

'two messuages and three yard lands [virgates] *and a quarter lying in Chalgrove aforesaid, two messuages and two yard lands lye in Langley and the other yard land and a quarter lye in the South field, and one parcel of meadow ground in Wydenham containing by estimation two acres with appurtenances thereunto belonging,'*

or

'a messuage and a close of pasture called the Home Close containing two acres and two parts of meadow lying in Mead Croft and Tuckney and 20 acres of land with the appurtenances lying in the common fields of Chalgrove also a parcel of close called Home Close containing one acre and nine acres of arable land lying in Chalgrove common fields and a close called Marsh Close containing by estimation three acres and one acre of meadow lying in Wydenham Mead with the appurtenances.' (Both Magdalen College.)

These descriptions remained the same throughout the centuries unless part of the property was sold, in which case that part was omitted and added to that of the purchaser's holding. Similarly, whereas in his will, 'Tudor John' could have said, *'.... John my sonn shale have ....'* a tenement, a messuage and eighteen acres of land in Bensington, Berrick, Roke and Ewelme, he describes each holding individually as *'.... one tenement in bensyngton with ix acreys of lande ....'* and *'.... to the same John one mesuage and ix acres of lande .... in ....bensyngton berwyke Roke and Ewelme ....'* and *'.... to richard my son one tenement .... with alle .... lands ....'* and *'my son shale have the tenement and gardeyne callyd Jacobbs ....'* instead of just two tenements and a garden.

The fact that John of Ascott's wife, Elizabeth, was included in the sale of the property referred to in the Feet of Fines, suggests that it had come from her family and that he had acquired it by way of marriage. For only in such circumstances were married women given the chance to participate in the transfer of property and, even then, it was a mere formality. We have seen from the Magdalen College manorial records, that whenever a man was selling a copyhold holding handed down through his wife's family, or was changing the lease, perhaps that it might pass to his own, she was *'.... first soley and secretly examined by ye Steward'* (1651) and *'... solely and separately examined apart from her said husband ....'* (1756). Yet how could she have opposed her husband's wishes? It was understood that whatever had once been hers, was now his, to do with as he chose. Indeed some men seem to have married simply to seize the property and did so straight away. Thus if the need arose for John of Ascott to sell the two messuages, a garden, the right to graze three cows and thirty-two acres of land, his wife had only to accompany him and be seen to be in agreement.

The Feet of Fines is dated within months of Edward VI, a Protestant King, having ascended the throne and, as national history often influenced our ancestors' lives, this may have been relevant. For those were troublesome times. King Henry had broken away from the Church, that he might divorce the Queen and marry Anne Boleyn and since then many of those who clung to the old religion, had been imprisoned or executed. The Reformation was taking place. Monasteries had been sacked and their property confiscated. Catholics were persecuted and lived in fear. Priest holes were constructed in larger houses, that a priest might celebrate the Mass in secret and be concealed whenever necessary. Those of John of Ascott's generation, having been brought up as good Catholics, would have remained true to their faith and as well as guarding against any threat to their family's safety, would have done whatever they could to ensure that their property was secure. Was that why a trusted and influential relative was chosen as the other party in the Feet of Fines? (For as John Rolles' grandson later became a courtier at the court of James I, another Protestant King, the family must have been highly regarded.) Perhaps John of Ascott had intended to repurchase the property when things were more settled, but if so, no record has survived. Or perhaps the £30 was needed in order to help bring about the marriage of his eldest son, as the two fathers would have had to have come to an agreement on monetary matters before the nuptials took place. In his will, dated 12th October 1549, Roger Quatermaine, who had witnessed 'Tudor John's' will, left the following bequest, *'Item to John Smyth by promesse to his mariage syxe pounde'*, which is explained by the marriage entry in the Chalgrove parish register, *'Anno 1549 ... John Smithe of Milton and Joane Catermaine were maried the XIXth day of May'*. (Ascott is in the parish of Great Milton.) Roger Quatermaine is thought to have been the leading inhabitant in Chalgrove at that time, as he was the only person eligible for taxation in the Lay Subsidy of 1549 and *'John Smyth the eldre'*, paying sixteen shillings for £16 in goods, was the only one in Ascott. The tax threshold must have been high that year, as is evident from those listed in other nearby parishes, for example, only two men in Little Haseley, both of whom were knights, and one, a gentleman, in Brightwell Baldwin. The fact that John of Ascott appears in the list as *'John Smyth the eldre'* shows that his son was still living there although he was not eligible for taxation. This is confirmed by the Lay Subsidy in the Spring of 1551, which shows John Smith Senior paying fourteen shillings for £14 worth of goods and John Smith Junior paying ten shillings for £10 worth of goods. They were the only two listed in this year and the next, the only difference being that the elder John had then acquired £16 worth of goods and was therefore paying another two shillings.

Turning to the manorial records, from which more information was gleaned, John of Ascott was in the Homage, the jurors chosen from amongst the tenants who attended the Manor Court of Roke and Berrick, on 2nd July 1548 and again on 14th August 1549. However, he was fined for not attending the court held on 16th July 1550 and a translation of the entry, written in Latin, reads, *'John Smyth, free suitor* (ie Freeholder) *owes suit and has not come'*. (Magdalen College.) We had already found a burial of a John Smith in the Great Milton parish register, on 6th November 1552, and therefore naturally assumed that John of Ascott had finally succumbed to whatever ailment had kept him from the Manor Court. His wife had presumably died between 1547 (the date of the Feet of Fines) and 1550 (the start of the parish register) as we could not find a burial entry relating to her. That of *'John Leyvendon father in lawe to John Smithe'*, in 1551, told us her maiden name though, as John of Ascott and his son were the only John Smiths in the parish at that time and the younger John had married the daughter of Roger <u>Quatermaine</u>.

What had happened to this young John thereafter, remained a matter for speculation. For the Lay Subsidy lists of 1551 and 1552 show that he was still in Ascott, but there were no more until 1559, by which time William and Nicholas Smith had inherited the property. It seemed likely that he had died without issue in another parish, as there were no possible burials in Great Milton or Chalgrove, and we wondered about a John Smith in Warborough and one in Brightwell Baldwin. But the latter was found in the Lay Subsidy list at the time that our John was named in that of Ascott, and both of the possibilities had surviving children, who would have inherited the property rather than William and Nicholas, and were thus ruled out. We were then working our way through the Court Books relating to Chalgrove, Berrick, Roke and Bensington and came to an entry, on 15th November 1559, written in Latin, which when translated read *'.... and that John Smith of Ascott who held of the lord of the manor certain free lands for a rent of 18 pence per annum has died since the last court'.* (Magdalen College.) It was as though the final piece of the puzzle had fallen into place. John, son of John of Ascott, <u>had</u> died between 1552 and 1559, but his burial had not been recorded. A careful study of the Great Milton parish register and those of Chalgrove and Brightwell Baldwin, revealed that there was a substantial increase in the number of burials in all three places in 1557, especially from March – June, which suggests that that part of Oxfordshire was probably in the grip of some sort of pestilence, such as plague or smallpox. It looks as if there was another outbreak in 1558, as the numbers were still high, particularly in August – September in Great Milton, which was within the period that young John of Ascott was said to have died, *'the last court'* referred to earlier, having been held on 14th March 1558. Was this why there was an oversight? For if he <u>was</u> a plague victim, he may have been taken from Ascott, in the southernmost part of the large parish of Great Milton, to the church, in the northernmost part, by night, in order to reduce the risk of contagion, and an ageing vicar, roused from his bed to perform the service, may have forgotten to record it the following morning. Alternatively, if the plague was widespread, he could have died whilst on a journey, to the market in Oxford perhaps, and would have been buried quickly wherever he was and because of his name, no one will ever know.

Another possible explanation stems from a law passed in 1598, compelling incumbents to copy the parish registers on to parchment, in order to preserve them, as they were written on poor quality paper. Tired eyes could thus have missed the odd one or two entries, especially at a time when some sort of pestilence had led to a substantial increase in the number of burials. Moreover, as John was such a common Christian name that in a 16th century tenant list only one man was called something other than that, if a string of them came together, the incumbent could easily have lost his place.

Whatever the answer, the missing burial had been accounted for and it seemed that John of Ascott had died in 1552 and his son about 1558, but on reading through the research, we suddenly realised something. There was only <u>one</u> entry (in Latin) which read, '.... *John Smith of Ascott who held of the lord of the manor certain free lands for a rent of 18 pence per annum has died since the last court'*. I have to admit that until Angela pointed this out, I had not thought of it, but I knew that she was right. For we had learnt enough from the manorial records to know that the Manor Court was only concerned with those who held land/property. Whatever happened to their families was not recorded, as it was of no importance. Thus, as the elder John of Ascott was the tenant, if <u>he</u> had died in 1552, the aforementioned entry would have appeared in the court book around that time, after which his son would have had to swear fealty at the Manor Court before becoming the tenant and a second entry would then have recorded his death in 1558/9. There was only <u>one</u> entry though, in 1558/9, which meant that the deaths were the other way around .... We then turned to the Lay Subsidy for Ascott and saw that, in 1559, William Smith was taxed on goods valued at £10 and Nicholas Smith on goods valued at £6, which added up to the £16 that their father was taxed on in the previous Lay Subsidy of 1552, whereas their brother had only had £10 worth of goods.

Having drawn up a beautiful family tree on several sheets of A1 size parchment-like paper, showing the 1552 date beneath the name of John of Ascott, we were reluctant to make an alteration, but the manorial records had proved without doubt that he had died in 1558/9, perhaps during an outbreak of plague, and it must therefore have been his eldest son who was buried in 1552. The property thus passed to younger sons, Nicholas and William Smith and the fact that it was divided between them suggests that there was once a will which has not survived, or that their father's wishes were made known by word of mouth. The next manor court following the announcement of his death, was held at about the time that Nicholas was married, which may have been why he and his brother did not attend. Although judging by the number of times that we read the words, *'Nicholas Smyth essoin through ....'* as he grew older, he can never have been keen to attend and perhaps William felt the same. ('Essoin through' meant that someone unable to attend, sent an excuse by way of another tenant in order to avoid paying a fine.) It was therefore at the court held on 13th August 1564, that the brothers were formally admitted to the property and the entries written in Latin, read,

> *'To this court came William Smith and certified himself a free tenant of the lord of the manor .... and pays 10 pence for 6 acres of land and 1 rod of land arable situated lying and being in the fields and parishes of Oke Berwik and Bensington in the county of Oxford whence 1 acre lies in Fowlstows and 5 [?] rods in Blacklands Furlong and 1 rod lies in Roke Croft [?] and 1½ acres lies in Whitelands and 1 acre in Stony Land on [?] the Knolle and 1 rod of land lies in a place there called Kings Ditch and he did fealty for the same.'*
> (Magdalen College.)

and

> *'To this court came Nicholaus Smith and certified himself a free tenant of the lord of this manor .... and pays 8 pence per annum for 1 messuage etc. in Roke within the [?] of Bensington in the county of Oxford situated and lying between the messuage of Magdalen College Oxford on the west and the messuage of Richard Hester on the south and the messuage of*

Robert Quelch on the east and the Queen's highway on the north and 6 acres and 3 rods of arable land with appurtenances dispersed in the fields of Bensington Roke and Berwyke and he did fealty for the same.' (Magdalen College.)

The aforementioned conclusions were subsequently corroborated by entries in the Lincoln College, Oxford, manorial records, which read, 12th October 1559, *'The Homage say upon their oath that John Smyth of Ascot and William Wise .... have died since the last court,'* and 17th October 1564, *'John Smythe who held of the lord for rent 8 pence died. A relief of 8 pence is due to the lord. Nicholas Smythe is his lawful heir.'* Again there were no entries relating to a John Smith in 1552, or thereabouts, and the naming of Nicholas Smith as the heir of John Smith of Ascott, shows that his eldest son, John, had already died.

The following entries, translated from the Latin, were taken from the Manor Court roll of the Court Baron of Lincoln College, Oxford, dated 19th September 1570:

'.... Nicholas Smyth holds freely a messuage in Rooke for 8 pence per annum. William Smyth holds freely etc. for 4 pence per annum ....'

'Homage of Barwycke and Rooke

Thomas Spyndeler	*Thomas Caterell*
William Vycary	*Nicholas Smyth*
William Spyndeler	*Thomas Quelche*
William More'	

'The homage present .... also that William Smyth is a free tenant and has defaulted in attendance therefore he is placed in mercy as appears' [fined sixpence].

Through the kindness of Nicholas's heart, both of his aforementioned freehold properties, held from Magdalen

College and Lincoln College, Oxford, eventually passed to his brother's grandson, John of Chalgrove, and provided us with the proof as to who he was. In trying to find this proof however, and thus bridge the gap between our earliest ancestors from Berrick Salome and Ascott and John of Chalgrove, in the days before the Ascott wills were discovered, we encountered what seemed to be an insurmountable problem, to which we have alluded, but which we have not yet commented upon. All of the early records are written in Latin. The catalogue listing those at the Magdalen College Archives, is in English and is therefore most helpful, as it contains abstracts of individual documents, but there is no such key to the contents of the Manor Court books, covering the period 1516 to 1733 (thereafter in English), which proved to be a treasure trove of information. Something had to be done about that, or our hands were tied, and Angela therefore turned to The National Archives website, an excellent resource for medieval Latin (which differs from classical Latin). Pages and pages of lessons were printed and put into a ring binder and, using this together with 'Manorial Records' – Denis Stuart, she resolutely taught herself the language, thereby unlocking the door to the remoter past. Before a visit to the Magdalen College Archives, she revised as if for an examination and slowly and steadily, we worked our way backwards through the great, leather-bound tomes, in search of another age and, as time went on and the handwriting became even harder to decipher, I found it fascinating that when confronted by a page covered with what might almost have been hieroglyphics, Angela could now reveal what lay hidden within! It was rather like weaving a tapestry. Each little piece of information was like a thread and whether this was a long-forgotten road name, a field name, the whereabouts of a house or cottage no longer there, or some event such as the marriage of someone from one of the families whom we had come to know, to someone from another perhaps, as these threads were interwoven, a little more colour was added to the picture which had begun to form of the village of Chalgrove as it once was. Moreover, we found our John Smith (John of Chalgrove) there, in his youth and amongst the later lists of tenants and as we reached back further, into the early 16th century, out from those pages stepped 'Tudor John'. Until then, we had only caught a glimpse of him in the words of the will, thus it was fascinating to see him there, going about his business, all those centuries ago. The documents show that he was typical of the 15th – early 16th century Husbandman, who later became known as a Yeoman, as described in the book entitled, *'The English Yeoman'* – Mildred Campbell, in that he bought and sold property throughout his lifetime, some of which he passed down through his sons, thus laying the foundations of a good standard of living. One of the earliest documents, a Rental and Memo re Tythes, dated 1503, told us that he held freehold lands of John Butler, Knight, in Berrick Salome, for which he was paying twenty-seven shillings per annum; that he was farming Magdalen College's own land at that time; and that both the messuage and virgate in Roke and the toft and virgate there, called Rolfes, which the college was then leasing to John Cottrell, had previously been in his tenure. Yet another reference to him was found in the 1497 court roll relating to Berrick and Roke, which lists all those with property in need of some repair. This last was therefore taken into account when estimating his date of birth during the 1470s. Having subsequently found his eldest son in the Lay Subsidy list of 1517 however, and estimated <u>his</u> date of birth at about 1490 or earlier, we thought it more probable that 'Tudor John' had been born between 1460 and 1470 and were looking for clues as to where.

Another document, dated 16th March 1504, records the purchase of *'a third part of one messuage with 21 acres lying in the towns and fields of Bensington, Roke,*

Berwyke and Ewelme', from William Beche of Thomley. This was then sold to Henry Spyndeler of Ewelme on 5th August 1509, perhaps as the other part of the messuage had remained tied up and 'Tudor John' thus felt that it was not worthwhile. Attached to the foot of this document was his seal and, quite coincidentally, it was a Tudor Rose ....

As time went on, two Chalgrove copyholders supposedly called John Smith appeared in the manorial records, but these turned out to be John Symmes Alias Smith Senior and Junior (forebears of the Roger Symmes in Chapter 8). They were variously referred to as Symmes Alias Smyth, Smyth Alias Symmes and as simply Symmes or Smyth, but by making use of the local history research, we were able to prove that in each instance it was one and the same person. For example, the list of tenants, taken from the Rentals, which applies to the messuage and half a virgate at Bower End reads:

1503 Thomas Planten (property late Thomas Gybbs)
pre 1520 John Smyth (property late Thomas Planten)
1520 John Symmes Junior (property late Thomas Gybbs)
1520 John Symmes the Younger (property late Thomas Gybbs)

and this tenant is also written as *'John ~~Smyth~~ Symmes Junior'* in the Court Book in 1518; whilst the elder one is shown as *'John Smyth Alias Symmes'* (1516), *'John Smyth Alias Symmes Senior'* (1517), *'John Symmes Alias Smyth Senior'* (1518), *'John Smyth Senior'* (1519), *'John Symmes'* (1523), has a will in the name of John Symmes and was buried as *'John Smyth'!* Fortunately, our own John Smythe was *'of Berwyke'* and that singled him out.

There must have been other transactions, the records of which have not survived, but we were fortunate in that he nevertheless appears in the court books, although not always for the right reasons! For example, on 18th July 1518, *'the tenth year of the reign of King Henry VIII'*, the entry reads, *'John Smythe of Berwyke ....'* [and others] *'.... freeholders in Berwyke, owe suit of court and have not come'*. He was to have been fined as a result of this, but must have turned up late, as a further entry at the same court reads,

'To this court came John Smythe of Berwyke and declared himself a free tenant of the lord'. He held *'a toft a close .... six acres and three rods of land with appurtenances in Roke and Berwyk which were late in the tenure of John Erly for rent of 14 pence per annum and he was admitted at the court and did fealty to the lord'.*

The entry *'John Smythe of Berwyk is a free tenant and owes suit of court'* on 21st June 1519, *'the eleventh year of the reign of King Henry VIII'*, tells us that he was again fined for not attending the manor court and although the examples shown are only brief entries, how they bring one's ancestor to life, by making him so much more than just a name on paper. Indeed, just to read the words *'.... in the tenth year of the reign of King Henry VIII ...'*, which refers to a time known only from what is written in the history books, and to know who someone in our family was, <u>where</u> he was and something of what he was doing then, is, in our opinion, truly fascinating.

To us, the Magdalen College archives and those held by Lincoln College, Oxford, are like hidden treasure and during our most recent expedition in search of this, we chanced upon a veritable gem under Freeholders of Berwyke in a Rental dated 1520, which reads:- *'John Smyth for the landes late Cowdreys by the Right of his wiff, daughter of Gyles Otherwyse called Aleyn'.* (Magdalen College.) Our first thought was that this refers to Agnes (named in the will of 'Tudor John', proved 1534). But does it? Or was there an Alice Cowdrey and was Agnes his second wife? That would explain why John of Ascott's eldest daughter was called Alice (will proved 1534) at a time when the first female child was usually named for her father's mother. Moreover, there must have been a big difference in the ages of John of Ascott and his brother, Richard, judging by the dates of their burials (1558 and 1593), even allowing for the fact that Richard lived to a great age. (Evident from the minimum age of his son at the time, this son having been named in the will proved 1534.) A second marriage would therefore account for the age gap, inasmuch as John may have been the son of Alice and Richard the son of Agnes. It may perhaps also be relevant that Roger Katermain (an early spelling of Quatermaine) was the first to witness the will of 'Tudor John', as a relative was often chosen to fulfil this role, usually a close relative. His age (estimated by taking into account the date that his will was proved, 1549, and the fact that he then had a daughter of marriageable age and a fifteen-year-old grandson) leads one to wonder whether he was 'Tudor John's' son-in-law. Having come from Chalgrove he was certainly not a neighbour and cannot have been just a friend, or he would not have been given precedence over John Mor, another of the witnesses, who is thought to have been related by marriage. (Remark *'my cousin, Leonard More'*, from the later will of Nicholas Smith.) Consequently if this assumption is correct, Roger's wife, <u>Alice</u>, would have been the daughter of 'Tudor John' – probably one of the elder ones, as that would have given her husband precedence over the husbands of any younger ones – and she may have been named for her mother .... In her will, proved 1559, she bequeathed a substantial sum of money to Maud <u>Smith</u>, whose relationship we are still trying to establish. At present, this is merely conjecture, but whilst any of the so-called 'hidden treasure' remains undiscovered, we are hopeful that Alice Cowdrey may one day take her place at the top of the tree, beside our earliest known, many times Great Grandfather.

The last entry in the Lincoln College manorial records relating to *'John Smyth of Berwyk who held of the lord freely'* tells us that he had died since the last court (ie between 7th October 1534 and 4th October 1535) and that *'John Smythe of Ascote is his son and heir'*. 'Tudor John' now lies within the hallowed walls of Chalgrove Church, near perhaps to his Great Great Grandson, John, who was to inherit part of his property, or perhaps to John's mother, Elizabeth, later Quatermaine, which seems a fitting end to the search. Fitting in that he left money to the church and to many more churches and chapels than anyone whose will we have read – to the Mother Church of Lincoln and those of Chalgrove, Ascott, Berrick Salome, Brightwell Baldwin, Stadhampton, Newington, Bensington, Ewelme, Watlington and Lewknor. As well as giving us an insight into his character, this is an indication of wealth and it seems that he may therefore find his way into the text of the forthcoming Volume 18 of the *Victoria County History*. The search has been full of surprises and this, together with the fact that three of our family are buried in the church there at Chalgrove, makes us so proud.

Where though do our roots lie? In the hope of finding some sort of clue, we turned once more to the manorial records and chanced upon a grant of land in Haseley, Chalgrove and Latchford in 1442, from William Quatermaine of Chalgrove to *'John Walkleyn of Overton'*, Brightwell Baldwin and *'John Smyth of the same'*. Of course, with a name like that, it could have been anyone. Except that Walkleyn is a most uncommon name in these parts. The only other one of that name whom we have come across, is bracketed together with 'Tudor John' as petty collectors of the Lay Subsidy for *'Barwyke, Overton and Balldelyn Bryghtwell'* in 1523. As an aside, the fact that 'Tudor John' was given this responsibility, shows that he was reliable and trustworthy and that he could read and count, as he was provided with a list showing the names of those to be taxed and the sums to be collected. The amount which he himself paid, enables us to gauge his status, in that whereas he was at the head of the list paying forty shillings (£2), which, at the rate of four pence in the pound, implies assets worth £120, the next highest amount was six shillings (30p), implying assets worth £18; whilst in Chalgrove, Roger Quatermaine, the close friend or relation who was later to witness his will, was at the head of that list, paying twenty shillings (£1- ie assets worth £60). The person chosen as the supervisor/ overseer of 'Tudor John's' will, was the John Walkelen in the Lay Subsidy list who, like the one in 1442, was from Brightwell Baldwin. It was always someone who could be relied upon to carry out the testator's wishes, who was chosen to be the supervisor/overseer and it was therefore usually someone in the family, who was not a legatee, who was given the responsibility, such as a brother-in-law or son-in-law. So was John Walkelen a relative? He could just have been a close friend, but as he was not living in the same parish, that seems unlikely. Moreover, John of Ascott and his brother, Richard, were the overseers of John Walkelen's will in 1534 and John of Ascott that of his widow in 1545, whilst Richard and his wife received a legacy. This close association with the family continued, Richard's son, John (buried 1611), having been chosen as the overseer of the will of Florence Alnote (formerly Spyer, née Walkelen), the daughter of John Walkelen, in 1597/8, which leads one to wonder whether her mother, Elizabeth Walkelen, was 'Tudor John's' sister. More importantly though, the fact that the John Walkelen who died in 1449, is likely to have been the grandfather of the one supervising 'Tudor John's' will, as they both came from Brightwell Baldwin and have a very uncommon surname, suggests that the *John Smyth of Overton'*, Brightwell Baldwin, together with whom he was granted land in 1442, was either the father or grandfather of 'Tudor John', depending upon his age. Of course there is no proof, but one small factor in favour of that, is that Richard Smith, younger son of 'Tudor John', was living in Brightwell Baldwin and had land in both Overtown and Nethertown. In the nearby churchyard are the headstones of his descendants and within the church a brass records the burial, beneath the medieval tiles, of one John ye Smythe, in 1371. An earlier ancestor perhaps? In view of the fact that 'Tudor John's' probable father or grandfather was from Overton, Brightwell Baldwin and that within about seventy years of the death of John ye Smythe, he was of an age to be leasing land, it certainly seems likely.

In his article entitled, 'John the Smith', Dr John Blair of Queen's College, Oxford, comments on how this 14th century Blacksmith made something of himself by buying property in the years following the Black Death (1348–9). This having wiped out a third of the population, there was so much available land and such a shortage of labour, that the serfs who had survived, found themselves in a strong position and were thus able to demand higher wages, for if one lord would not pay, another would. This therefore enabled many to buy their freedom and acquire property and status. Such was the social climate when John ye Smythe was setting aside a little with which to purchase freehold land once owned by those who had succumbed to the Bubonic Plague. 'Tudor John' seems to have been just as enterprising, so were they related and did he once come along the ancient track known as Hollandtide Bottom, which runs from Brightwell Baldwin to Berrick Salome (Berwyke), in search of freehold land – the land which was to lead us to him, centuries later? If only we knew .... There are no signposts though, to the remoter past. No baptisms, marriages, burials, nor even proper surnames prior to the 15th century, other than those relating to the most powerful families. Thus those whom we have encountered amongst the well-kept manorial records held by Magdalen College, have no proof of who they were and yet, inasmuch as they were living in the hamlets where our people are known to have been, perhaps handing their trade on from father to son, they COULD be our ancestors and it is fascinating to picture them there, centuries and centuries ago ....

Robert the Smith of *'Holecumbe'*, but a stone's throw from Berwyke, and Norgany, his wife, for example. In 1354, having somehow survived the Black Death, or Bubonic Plague, they were receiving a grant of land in *'Bensyntone'*, to the west of *'Ewelleweye'*, in the *'field of Roke'*, the very same land which had been purchased by Richard le Smyth of Bensyntone, two years earlier. A further grant of land, this time in Berewyk, was made to Robert and Norgany the following year. This was situated near to that of Sir Hugh de Berewyk, the Vicar of Brightwell Baldwin (in 1333). Then in 1356, they were granted more land in 'Bensyntone', again near that of Sir Hugh and this transaction was witnessed by Richard the Smith. The other witness was Roger Gerard and working our way backwards, we see that in 1339, Richard the Smith of 'Bensyntone', his wife, Joan, and their daughter, Emma, were receiving a grant of arable land in 'Bensyntone', beside that of Roger Gerard.

There was a John le Smith witnessing a grant of the Bolt family of Berewyk in 1316 and the land referred to, was situated beside that which was granted to Robert and Norgany in 1355. This earlier deed therefore provides a link between John le Smith and both Richard and Robert, and leads one to wonder whether he could be the one who is mentioned in the Cuxham manorial records 'for trespass with 40 sheep' in the common cornfield and on the lord's land, in 1355 and 1356, whose brass plaque in St Bartholomew's Church, Brightwell Baldwin, records his passing in 1371, and to wonder also whether he was perhaps the father, grandfather or uncle of one or both of them. Some sort of relationship certainly seems likely. Moreover, the fact that Richard made a grant of land to Robert, may mean that he was his father and that the grant was made on the occasion of his marriage. For, similarly, 'Tudor John' made a grant to his son, Richard, in the 16th century, probably at the time of his marriage, and later left the property to him in his will, in his own words, 'accordyng to the graunt made to hym and hys heres by me and Agnes my wyffe'.

The Smiths were the first freemen. Paid for their services to the nobility and gentry, they were able to buy their freedom from serfdom and thereafter to put their monies to good use by building up a tenement of holdings. One of the first to do so, was perhaps John de Ock ('of the oak', from which the place name Roke was derived), the Smith, who in 1280 or earlier, at about the time that Edward I was forming the first Parliament and setting out the laws of the land, was witnessing a deed and purchasing arable land at *'Oke'*. Richard and Robert in the 14th century, had land in *'the field of Roke'* and the property which passed on through our family from the will of 'Tudor John', was also in Roke. Thus it seems that our roots lie there, in that quiet corner of Oxfordshire, at the foot of an ancient oak perhaps, and finding our way there from those tangled beginnings amid the sad streets of 19th century Croydon, has been a journey through Time, which has enriched our lives.

Of course the most momentous occurrence was the arrival of the letter from Firepower, without which none of this could have been written, but there were other unforgettable moments, which were like milestones along our way – when Rachel Simon solved the mystery of *'Sarton'* Lee .... the signature of John of Chinnor on a Settlement Certificate .... the probate of John the Wheelwright, which gave our family status .... the realisation that the Elizabeth Smith who had married Robert Quatermaine, was the mother of John of Chalgrove .... and the wills of Nicholas Smith and 'Tudor John', which finally forged the link and brought our journey into the past to an end.

But as I prepare to put down my pen, the search goes on. For when following the long-ago lanes revealed to us by those great, leather-bound tomes wherein the Chalgrove of centuries past lies hidden, we sometimes catch a glimpse of our forefathers, who have come to mean so much to us. Even the merest mention of them in a document brings them closer and can conjure the distant rumble of an iron-shod cart, or a whispered word from another Time .... a Time from which has sprung a tree of vast proportions, which records the names of more than a thousand yeomen, husbandmen, wheelwrights, agricultural labourers, carpenters, soldiers, servants, lacemakers, gamekeepers, carters, sawyers, lace beaders, a stonecutter, a gentleman, a drover, a jockey, an alehouse keeper, a carrier, a builder's labourer, a weaver, a sheep farmer, a footman, a carman, a cordwainer, a chauffeur, a tailor, a shoemaker, a golf groundsman, a brewer, a painter, a postman, a chair maker, a waggoner, a shepherd, a farmer, a sandstone miner, a platelayer, a laundress, a ploughman, a bricklayer, an ostler, a mill hand, a Colour Sergeant and an acting Quartermaster Sergeant in the Royal Field Artillery .... every one of whom was a part of our supposedly small family(!)

It is therefore somewhat startling to think of all that may have been lost, had the bus arrived but a few minutes late, or the film commenced at an earlier time, on that Friday evening so long ago ....

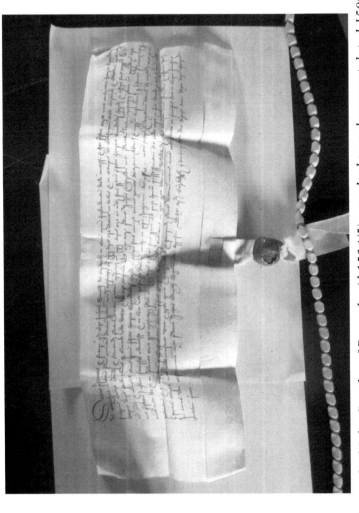

The seal of John Smythe of Berwyke (d.1534/5) attached to a document dated 1509. Chalgrove 108. By kind permission of The President and Fellows of Magdalen College, Oxford.

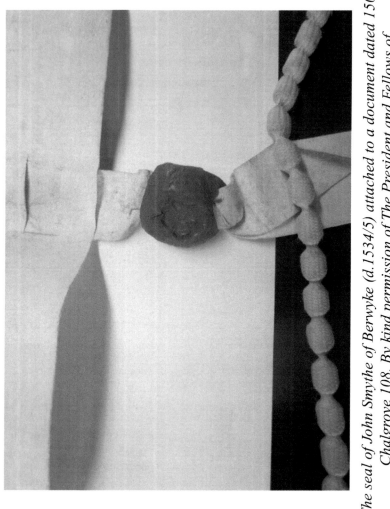

The seal of John Smythe of Berwyke (d.1534/5) attached to a document dated 1509. Chalgrove 108. By kind permission of The President and Fellows of Magdalen College, Oxford.

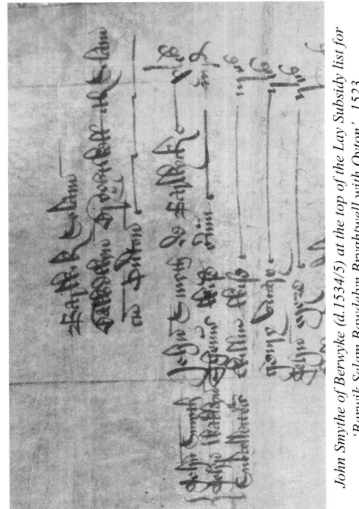

*John Smythe of Berwyke (d.1534/5) at the top of the Lay Subsidy list for
'Barwik Selam Bawdelyn Bryghtwell with Ovton', 1523.
Reproduced by kind permission of The National Archives.*

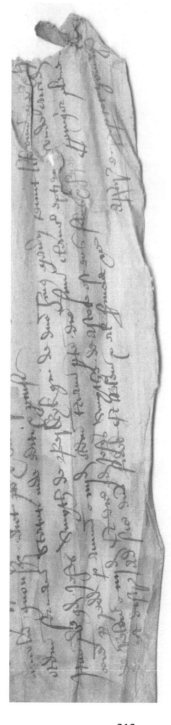

The entry in the Lincoln College, Oxford, manorial records recording the death of John Smythe of Berwyke in 1534/5 and naming John Smyth of Ascott as his son and heir: M/CHG/6. By kind permission of the Rector and Fellows of Lincoln College, Oxford.

St Mary's Church, Chalgrove, wherein John Smythe of Berwyke (d.1534/5), John Smith of Chalgrove (1601–79) and Elizabeth Quatermaine, formerly Smith, née Wise (1575–1670) are buried.

The medieval wall paintings recently uncovered in the chancel of St Mary's Church, Chalgrove – visible when John Smythe of Berwyke was laid to rest in the church, but whitewashed over before John Smith of Chalgrove and his mother were buried there.

POSTSCRIPT

Since this was completed, part of Volume 18 of the *Victoria County History* has been drafted and both John Smythe of Berwyke (d.1534/5) and John Smith of Chalgrove (1601–1679) are named therein as Freeholders.

BIBLIOGRAPHY AND REFERENCES

The Eureka Partnership. Books listed in Chapter 6 and a great many other titles available from www.eurekapartnership.com

Buckinghamshire Dialect – H. Harman. S. R. Publishers Ltd, 1970.

Catholicism and Community in Early Modern England – Michael C. Questier. Cambridge University Press, 2006.

Chinnor in Camera – Mary Darmody-Cadle and Pat Whelehan. Baron Books of Buckingham, 2000.

Discovering Your Family History – Don Steel. BBC, 1980.

Index to the Probate Records of the Courts of the Bishop and Archdeacon of Oxford, 1733–1857 and of the Oxfordshire Peculiars, 1547-1856 – (editors) D. M. Barratt, Joan Howard-Drake and Mark Priddey. The British Record Society, Volume 109, 1997.

In Search of Ancestry – Gerald Hamilton-Edwards. Phillimore & Co. Ltd, 1974, reprinted 1979 (first pub. Michael Joseph Ltd, 1966).

Manorial Records – Denis Stuart. Phillimore & Co. Ltd, 1992.

Manorial Records of Cuxham, Oxfordshire, circa 1200–1359 – (editor) P. D. A. Harvey. Oxfordshire Record Society and HMSO, Volume 50, 1976.

Oxford Church Courts Depositions – Jack Howard-Drake. Oxfordshire County Council.
    1542–1550 pub. 1991.
    1570–1574 pub. 1993.
    1581–1586 pub. 1994.
    1589–1593 pub. 1997.
    1592–1596 pub. 1998.
    1603–1606 pub. 1999.
    1609–1616 pub. 2003.
    1629–1634 pub. 2007.
    1634–1639 pub. 2008.

Oxfordshire Contributors to the Free and Voluntary Present to King Charles II, 1661 – Jeremy Gibson. Oxfordshire Family History Society in association with the Family History Partnership, 2012.

Politics and Loyalty in Post-Revolution Oxfordshire: The 1690 County Parliamentary Poll; the Association Oath Rolls, 1695–6 – Jeremy Gibson. Oxfordshire Family History Society in association with the Family History Partnership, 2011.

Probate Records of the Courts of the Bishop and Archdeacon of Oxford, 1516–1732, Volume 1, A–K – D. M. Barratt. The British Record Society, Volume 93, 1981.

Probate Records of the Courts of the Bishop and Archdeacon of Oxford, 1516–1732, Volume 2, L–Z – D. M. Barratt. The British Record Society, Volume 94, 1985.

The Dictionary of Genealogy – Terrick V. H. FitzHugh. Alphabooks, 1986.

The English Yeoman – Mildred Campbell. The Merlin Press, London, 1983.

The King's England, Buckinghamshire – (editor) Arthur Mee. Hodder & Stoughton Ltd, London, 1943.

The Papers of Captain Henry Stevens, Waggon-Master-General to King Charles I – (editor) Margaret Toynbee. Oxfordshire Record Society, Volume 42, 1961.

The Place-names of Buckinghamshire – A. Mawer and F. M. Stenton. Cambridge University Press, first pub. 1925, reissued 1969. English Place-name Society, Volume 2.

The Village Labourer – J. L. and Barbara Hammond. Pearson Education Limited. © Professor N. Hammond and Pearson Education, 1966.

ABBREVIATIONS FOR REPOSITORIES

CBS   –   Centre for Buckinghamshire Studies.
HRO   –   Hampshire Record Office.
MofC   –   Museum of Croydon.
OHC   –   Oxfordshire History Centre.
SHC   –   Surrey History Centre.
TNA   –   The National Archives.
WSRO –   West Sussex Record Office.

PARISH REGISTERS

St James, Croydon Common, West Croydon – SHC. 2809/1/3 and 2809/1/14.

Leigh – SHC. 2869/1/1.

Holmwood – SHC. HO/1/1 and HO/1/7.

Capel – SHC. CAP/1/3, CAP/4/1 and CAP/3/1.

Ashtead – SHC. ATDGIL/3/1.

Dorking – SHC. DOM/1/7, DOM/2/3, DOM/3/1 and DOM/3/2.

Horsham – WSRO. PAR106/1/2/1, PAR106/1/2/2 and PAR106/1/1/5.

Saunderton – CBS. PR179/1/2.

Bledlow – CBS. PR17/1/3.

Lacey Green – CBS. PR122/1/3.

Chinnor – OHC. PAR63/1/R1/2 and PAR63/1/R1/3.

St Mary Magdalen, Oxford – OHC. PAR208/1/R1/3.

Chalgrove – OHC. PAR57/1/R1/1 and PAR57/1/R1/2.

Great Milton – OHC. PAR171/1/R1/1.

Brightwell Baldwin – OHC. PAR40/1/R1/1 and PAR40/1/R1/2.

Drayton St. Leonard – OHC. PAR89/1/R1/1.

Pyrton – OHC. MS.d.Par.Pyrton e.7

Marriages, baptisms and burials databases of the Buckinghamshire Family History Society (www.bucksfhs.org.uk).

Marriages, baptisms and burials databases of the Oxfordshire Family History Society (www.ofhs.org.uk).

SCHOOLS RECORDS

Sydenham Road Junior Mixed School admission register, 1889–98 – MofC. SCH17/4/2/1.

Sydenham Road School logbook, 1895–7 – MofC. SCH135/1/1/2.

Woodside Junior School admission register, 1891–1904 – MofC. SCH158/2/7.

Woodside School logbook – MofC. SCH158/1/5.

Leigh School logbook, 1862–81 – SHC. CES/55/1.

LAY SUBSIDIES (TNA)

1517	–	E179/161/167.
1523	–	E179/161/198.
1543	–	E179/162/225.
1546	–	E179/162/250.
1547	–	E179/162/258.
1549	–	E179/162/274.
1551	–	E179/162/288.
1552	–	E179/162/301.
1559	–	E179/162/322.
1568	–	E179/162/331.
1577	–	E179/162/341.
1581	–	E179/162/346.
1594	–	E179/163/381.
1599	–	E179/163/394.

WILLS AND PROBATE

Alnote, Florence – OHC. 190.312.
Beckley, Letitia – OHC. 117/1/36.
Bedford, Agnes – OHC. 183.197.
Bigg, Mary – OHC. 8/5/10.
Edwards, John – TNA. PROB 11/207/15.
Goode, Jeffrey – OHC. 28/3/20.
Keene, Elizabeth – TNA. PROB 11/828/420.
Quatermaine, Alice – OHC. 183.284.
   Joane – OHC. 54/3/14.
   Olive – OHC. 54/3/18.
   Robert – OHC. 54/4/3.
   Roger – OHC. 180.10.
   William – OHC. 146/4/6.
Rolles, Thomas – TNA. PROB 11/108/443.
Simeon, Richard – OHC. 58/1/41.
Smith, George – OHC. 150/2/35.
  John (1534) – OHC. 178.108.
  John (1582) – OHC. 187.135.
  John (1603) – OHC. Pec. 50/5/26.
  John (1611) – OHC. 59/1/24.
  John (1637) – OHC. 173/4/6.
  John (1679) – OHC. 62/1/14.
  John (1705) – OHC. 63/1/21.
  John (1757) – OHC. Ta. iv/xxviii/4.
  Nicholas – OHC. Pec. 51/1/1a.
  Richard (1568) – OHC. 184.350.
  Richard (1577) – OHC. 185.501.
  Richard (1593) – OHC. 189.214 and 173/2/8.
  William (1605) – OHC. Pec. 50/5/22.
  William of Gt Marlow (1726) – CBS. DA/WF 75/23.
Stevens, Edward – OHC. 149/1/15
Symmes, John – OHC. 179.57
Walkelen, Elizabeth – OHC. 179.64
  John – OHC. 178.101
Wildgoose, Raynold – OHC. 70/1/21

MANORIAL RECORDS

The entries translated from the Latin are our own translations.

Lincoln College, Oxford

Court rolls – M/CHG/6, M/CHG/8 and M/CHG/10.
Minutes – M/CHG/19, M/CHG/21 and M/CHG/32.
Presentments – M/CHG/28, M/CHG/52, M/CHG/63 and M/CHG/91.
Lists of Suitors – M/CHG/232-241.

Magdalen College, Oxford

Court books – ECB/4, ECB/6, ECB/45, ECB/58 and EP/142/14.
Court rolls – EP/122/4 and EP/81/29.
Rentals – EP/142/28, EP/142/9, D-Y295, Chalgrove 276.
1822 Survey – CP3/20 and MP/1/57.
Grants – Chalgrove 18b, Chalgrove 37b, Chalgrove 42b, Chalgrove 46a, Chalgrove 47b, Chalgrove 49b, Chalgrove 105, Chalgrove 108, Chalgrove 260 and Chalgrove 274.

CENTRE FOR BUCKINGHAMSHIRE STUDIES

Settlement certificates – PR4/13/2/77 (Smith, Amersham/Chinnor) and PR176/13/1/59 (Smith, Princes Ris./Monks Ris.)

HAMPSHIRE RECORD OFFICE

Indenture, Bulkeley/Stevens – 1M53/1414.

OXFORDSHIRE HISTORY CENTRE

Land Tax assessments – QSD.L.64 and QSD.L.75
Chinnor tythe award and map – 95/A and 95/M
'Pages' deeds – Ta.iv/xxviii/1-17 and Li./v/iii

THE NATIONAL ARCHIVES

Feet of Fines 1547 – CP25/2/62/493.
1798 Land Tax, Oxfordshire – IR23/69.
Land Tax Exoneration Certificate – IR24/26 contract 14948.
Returns of the army – WO73/97-116.
1910 valuation assessment books – IR58/25071, IR58/25075 and IR58/25064.